BEST CANADIAN ESSAYS 2014

Best Canadian Essays 2014

EDITED BY Christopher Doda

AND Natalie Zina Walschots

TIGHTROPE BOOKS

2015

Tightrope Books
#207—2 College Street
Toronto, ON M5G 1K3
www.tightropebooks.com

SERIES EDITOR: Christopher Doda
GUEST EDITOR: Natalie Zina Walschots
MANAGING EDITOR: Heather Wood
COVER DESIGN: Deanna Janovski
TYPOGRAPHY: Carleton Wilson

We thank the Canada Council for the Arts and the Ontario Arts Council
for their support of our publishing program.

Canada Council **Conseil des Arts**
for the Arts **du Canada**

ONTARIO ARTS COUNCIL
CONSEIL DES ARTS DE L'ONTARIO
an Ontario government agency
un organisme du gouvernement de l'Ontario

PRINTED AND BOUND IN CANADA

A cataloguing record for this publication is available from Library and
Archives Canada.

Contents

Introduction

ANYONE WHO HAS read the series *Best Canadian Essays* for the last five years will have undoubtedly noticed that we have used the term 'essay' in a rather liberal fashion. The classic definition of the essay, from Michel de Montaigne and Francis Bacon onwards, amounts to something like a free mind at play that meditates upon a specific subject with a hopeful intent to illuminate the reader as to that subject's inner workings. The 'classical' essayists' writing ranged from Shakespeare to drunkenness to cannibalism to why fathers love their children. In a society of taboos, the essay was a window into understanding human experience that was not easily spoken.

At first blush, it appears we have used the term in a broader sense. Over the first five years, we have published works that roam from political treatises to straight-forward journalism to philosophical meditations to personal remembrances to ruminations on art, music or literature, to scientific discourses to economic tracts. All have found a home under the rubric of 'Best Canadian Essays.' We have kept open the definition so as not to exclude any quality piece of writing just because it does not entirely conform to the classic definition the essay. Perhaps a more accurate sobriquet would be 'Best Canadian Non-fiction' but we are more interested in expanding the definition of the essay itself. The essay should be an inclusive, not an exclusive form: it can hold a multiplicity of not only opinion but style and variety in its expression. In fact, with the proliferation of online essay sites, some specific and some general, the essay has never had a broader audience or range of subject matter. Or as Andrew O'Hagan wrote in the *Telegraph* in London, "The modern essay can be a piece of work as personal as a love letter, as world-altering as a policy, capturing the spirit of the age in words that can seem to clear the air for new ways of living. Yet some of the best essays act like whispers for your ears alone.... And in the end that is what the essay gives you – a word in your ear and a thought before bedtime, all the better to speed your dreams and awaken your appetite for life." A little bit heady, but he is right in that these days the essay can really be about anything at all. (This tendency is even open for mockery. Recently the satirical news site *The Onion* proclaimed a 'cover story' on "'The Microfridge, an Essay on This Timeless Dorm Room Appliance' by Pulitzer Prize Winning Author Philip Roth.") He is also right in that essay can be transformative on a number of levels, whether it changes the outlook of a society or its effects remain localized to a small group or even an individual.

In our selection this year, we have borne that in mind. We surveyed a great deal of magazines and journals, as well as online content to arrive at the selection that appears before you here. And true to form, we've got pieces that are intensely personal, such as Eugene Stickland's article on palliative care and his dying father, Richard Teleky's need to rediscover fiction or Stacey May Fowles' memoir about her youth in the Scarborough area of Toronto, when the Scarborough Rapist, later revealed to be serial killer

Paul Bernardo, was stalking the streets. The same personal qualities infuse Daniel Scott Tysdal's "Year Zero," about the death of a former student, and Marion Agnew's "Words," about her mother's struggle with Alzheimer's disease. We have two articles of a very different nature, by Margo Pfeiff and Naomi Lewis, on the difficulties of scientific practice in Canada as Stephen Harper's government has moved away from evidence-based legislation. Similar government policies are examined by Kate Taylor in reference to the politicization of museums. There are a couple of calls to action in the form of Ezra Winton's demand for more activist filmmaking and Aaron Broverman's exposition on real-life Canadian costumed do-gooders. There's Ann Shin's article on the perils involved in making her film *The Defector*, about escapees from North Korea, a document about a documentary as it were. Sarah de Leeuw's remembrances are also nominally about film but eventually turn to matters of life and death. Lewis MacLeod provides a meditation on genius – and the public's perception of genius – with Bob Dylan as an example, a curious choice from a pair of avowed heavy metal fans like us. Kilby Smith-McGregor's piece is about genius as well, this time of the literary variety. D.W. Wilson provides some caustic thoughts on the over-analyzed but misunderstood notion of voice in fiction. And there's even a first for *Best Canadian Essays*: a book review. Heather Cromarty's thoughts on Amber Dawn's *How Poetry Saved My Life* are a staging ground for her reflections on the place of women in the literary world. So there's a great deal to pick from and learn from. More even than other years, this volume contains work by authors better known for work in other genres or media. This seems to suggest not that authors from other genres are turning to non-fiction but rather that all forms of creative expression offer knowledge, or if we're lucky wisdom, about the country (and world) in which we live.

As always, reading and compiling this volume has been a pleasure. We'd like to thank Tightrope's outgoing publisher Halli Villegas for giving us the opportunity in the first place. And we'd like to thank the incoming publisher Jim Nason, plus Heather Wood, and everyone currently at Tightrope Books for soldiering on.

– *Christopher Doda and Natalie Zina Walschots*

BEST CANADIAN ESSAYS 2014

Words

MARION AGNEW

IN MID-DECEMBER, 1997, I stood at my kitchen table, flipping through the mail. Among the bills and ads, I found a couple of Christmas cards.

"Hey, this one's from Mom," I said aloud. The card showed a sprig of mistletoe tied with a red ribbon. Under the printed greeting inside, Mom had signed "Jeanne" instead of her usual "Mother," and Dad had written, "Come see us! Ted." On the opposite page, Mom had written a note. As I read it, my stomach tightened.

I wish I had a time to visit together your during the avation. I enjoy very much some of the value evated as she sees us all. We enjoy very muh. I wish that all those precess that seem to have great help. Reap and the children are looking fast. Our children can "take forst" but we are working like greeting trying to see you again soon!

I winced. When did she get this bad?

For ten months, since Mom's diagnosis the previous February, I'd had a name for her forgetfulness and confusion, her lost and mangled words. Until then, my sister and I had simply called it "how she is," as in "you know how she is." But even after her diagnosis, I'd allowed "probable Alzheimer's disease" to remain an abstraction, separate from the woman who was my mother.

This Christmas card, shaking slightly in my hand, showed me her disease – right here, blue ink on white paper.

I sagged into a chair, blinking away tears to examine the card. She had really worked at this note, adding the word "your" to the first sentence: "I wish I had a time to visit together *your* during the avation." Did it make sense to her then?

As I looked, my initial horror became embarrassment. My father had no memory problems – why had he let her send this? Why had he let her *expose* herself in this way? My embarrassment turned into blaming annoyance at him, at his illegible scrawl. I looked again at what he'd written: "Come see us!"

Then I heard him – really heard him. *Come see us.* It was neither a command nor a demand; they were not his style. It was a plea beamed into the universe: "Is anyone there? Can anyone help us?" I felt the 800 miles between my home and theirs and sputtered sudden, guilty tears.

MOST PEOPLE THINK Alzheimer's disease is the same as memory loss. Well, *most* people don't think about Alzheimer's at all, if they can help it. Perhaps if we all ignore it hard enough, it will go away.

That was certainly my hope, even after I knew my mother's diagnosis. After all, I was still young, just in my thirties, with my own life concerns. My parents, who had been in their early forties when I was born, had always been satisfactory support for each other, their lives highly structured and extremely private. My four siblings and I had never spoken seriously and specifically with them about their money (that would be vulgar) or their health (that would be impertinent). Doing something active in relation to

4

my mother's forgetfulness and agitation felt unthinkable, impossible. On the rare occasions I let myself wonder about her health, I wanted to go to bed and pull the covers over my head.

But now, I had to think about this disease. Learn about it.

As Mom walked down the path of her disease, words dropped behind her – names here, a noun there. The farther into the disease she went, the more quickly the words disappeared, swirling behind her like autumn leaves caught strong wind. So I took that as my starting point: words. As Mom lost them, I would learn new ones.

After the holidays, I finally forced myself to read the neurologist's diagnostic report from the previous year, which my father had shared with my siblings and me.

Patient has some problems with verbal communication, but no aphasia or paraphasias are noted. She did have some apraxia…. Mini-mental status examination reveals a dismal score of 5/30.

From the dictionary, I learned that *aphasia* is a general inability to understand words and that *paraphasia* is the substitution of inappropriate words when speaking. *Apraxia* meant that Mom couldn't complete complex coordinated movements easily.

I already knew the meaning of the word *dismal.*

So, no aphasia or paraphasia? The neurologist's assessment contradicted Mom's Christmas note. Still, I had noticed that she could still speak relatively well at the social level: "Hi, how are you? Good to see you" were all phrases still close to the surface for her. Maybe the neurologist hadn't pushed the conversation beyond that level.

Or maybe Mom's abilities had deteriorated significantly in the year since this assessment. *Dismal.*

On further neuropsychological testing, the patient failed in all major areas. She did very poorly on orientation, very poorly on attention. She could not do calculation very well but this was actually better than most other areas.

My mother, born to a schoolteacher, started her formal schooling at the age of five in Grade Two. The teacher said to her, "The earth is shaped like an orange, slightly flattened at both ends. Now, can you say that back to me?"

My mother replied, "The earth is an oblate spheroid." She was moved into Grade Three immediately.

She graduated from high school at fifteen. At twenty-four, she earned a Ph.D. in mathematics. After World War II, she declined an invitation to move to Los Alamos, New Mexico, to pursue nuclear research. Instead, she married my father – a historian – raised a family of five; and became a university professor, teaching and conducting research in applied mathematics and mathematics education.

This neuropsychological test, which my mother took at the age of seventy-nine, may have been one of the few tests she ever failed.

AFTER READING THE diagnostic report, I knew what to do next: research. My professor parents had trained me well.

I learned that memory is only one of the losses in people with Alzheimer's. In fact, "loss" is the overarching theme. Early in the disease, patients lose their car in the parking lot or lose track of what they meant to say. Later, they lose their roles in life: husband? daughter? parent? At the end, they lose motivation. Awareness of their surroundings. Consciousness.

Some fourteen years after my mother's "probable" diagnosis, physicians still have no objective way to classify patients into stages, no T-cell or white blood cell count to mark thresholds. At that time, a positive diagnosis of

Alzheimer's required an analysis of brain tissue. In other words, an *autopsy*.

So Mom's neurologist estimated. According to his calculations, my mother had been lurking in the early stages of the disease (confusion, some word loss) for some seven years. Recently, she had slid into the middle stage, with its *sundowning* (night wakefulness), *wandering* (compulsive and anxious walking), and *rummaging* (obsessively searching for unknown items). Her confusion and antagonism would only increase.

I learned that as Mom's disease progressed, she would probably hallucinate. She would not only see and hear things that weren't there – her senses of taste and smell might become involved. We could expect only her sense of touch to remain relatively unchanged. Aside from a ceremonial hug and kiss at arrivals and departures, my family didn't touch much. But after my reading, I began putting my hand on her arm or shoulder every chance I got.

And I made more chances to see them. Before receiving that Christmas card, I'd visited my parents just twice a year. I saw them six times before the next Christmas holiday. Travelling the 800 miles between my home and theirs, even flying, chewed up most of a day each way. For each visit, I took a four- or five-day weekend and usually travelled alone or occasionally with Sue, my sister.

Fortunately, my boss was very understanding. I used all my vacation days, my "personal days," and even sick leave for days I went to doctor's appointments with them. Difficult as these visits were, there was nowhere else I would have gone, nowhere else I would rather have been.

After a trip, people always asked, "So did you have fun visiting your parents?"

The question stumped me. I didn't want to lie and just

say "yes." I wanted everyone, everywhere to know that smart, capable people got Alzheimer's disease. I wanted everyone to know just a little of what my mother was going through, what it was like for my father and the family – but most people didn't *really* want to know. And I didn't want to embarrass either my mother or my father. I just wanted to tell some of the truth – but not so much that I drove people away.

So of course my visits weren't *fun*, not even according to my own parents' definition of fun activities – long conversations at the table after a meal, going to a college athletic event, working desultorily at a 1000-piece jigsaw puzzle as an excuse for more chatting, looking at family photo albums, singing at the piano. As Mom's abilities diminished, our activities changed. I picked small jigsaw puzzles that she could finish in about a half-hour, with my surreptitious help, to forestall her frustration and agitation. I spent a lot of time distracting Mom so that her constant, confused questions didn't send my father's understandable irritation over the edge into angry shouting, which upset all of us.

Throughout my visits, I blocked out the memory of the inquisitive, intelligent woman Mom had been to focus on who she still was: *Mom Now*.

I also couldn't think of these visits as the opposite of *fun*, whatever that might be. For one thing, they stretched ahead of me for the foreseeable future. And for another, beyond them lay only a future in which I didn't have even *Mom Now* to visit.

Eventually, I settled on another word: *rewarding*. "I had a rewarding time," I would say, adding, "Mom and I made cookies together." Or "Mom and I went shopping." Or "Mom and I were in the kitchen and she said she was glad I was there." *Rewarding* came to encompass everything I couldn't say.

WHILE VISITING MY parents, I felt as if I were picking my way through a swamp at midnight, with dangers lurking in every direction.

Confronting some dangers only required me to grow up a little. I braved the family taboo on discussing money to learn that my parents' pensions adequately covered their expenses. I made lists of Mom's doctors and medications. After screwing up my courage, I asked to speak directly with my mother's doctors, even without her or my father present. My father wanted to give my mother good report cards, but the doctors needed to know what her abilities really were.

In fact, I found that confronting my father – gently but consistently – was the most dangerous and frightening part of this time. He was my mother's *caregiver*, a murky role that's something less than *nurse* and very different from *husband*. He had never been skilled in the practical tasks of caring and comforting, and he lacked patience. He couldn't accept that my mother couldn't learn and, in fact, would keep losing cognitive skills – her ability to focus on a book (and, later, to read), to distract herself from unhappy thoughts (later, to express them clearly), to watch an entire movie (later, to understand what she saw). She was not the woman he married, not the woman she'd become during their fifty years together.

She resisted bathing. She wore the same clothes, including underwear, day after day, and refused to discuss it with him. Worst of all, she couldn't recognize him as her husband. Some evenings she became scandalized, outraged at his expectation that she would sleep in their double bed. His response: shouting.

My father was angry: at the illness, at himself for not being able to cure her, at her for slipping away. He was angry at me for bearing witness to his short temper, for suggesting he comfort or indulge her when his inclination was to argue her "back to reality" – a trip she could not make. I was frightened of his anger, and I was plenty angry, too – angry that he wanted help and then wouldn't accept it. Angry that I wasn't doing enough, though I was doing all I could.

Aside from two extremely tense phone conversations, we didn't argue (that would have been vulgar) but we disagreed, and we knew we disagreed.

I kept reading – memoirs by caregivers, John Bayley's *Elegy for Iris*, memoirs by those in early-stage Alzheimer's. Nowhere could I find the book my father and I both needed so desperately – the one with the cure to my mother's illness, that would give her back to us.

BETWEEN CHRISTMAS OF 1997 and April of 1999, simply watching the modulations of my mother's life gave everyday words a new texture and colour.

The obvious: *Inexorable, inevitable, erosion, diminish.*

Ambivalence: After every visit, I hated yet was relieved to go.

Mixed blessing: Still having a mother to visit, but not the same mother I had known.

Bittersweet: Particularly when she and I, side-by-side in the middle of some simple activity, laughed together.

Sometimes *triumph, achievement*. My mother hummed the tunes as we watched an old musical together. My father had a nap while she and I chatted. At the breakfast table, she said she was delighted to see me.

Even *victory*. We made it through another day.

IN APRIL 1999, my mother experienced seizures and spent a month in the hospital. The seizures, said the neurologist, marked her descent into the late stage of Alzheimer's. My mother lost the ability to act independently. Reminding her to eat drew only her impassive stare, but if fed, she'd eat with pleasure. Similarly, she could walk with a walker if she had a friendly, encouraging face backing up in front of her, but without it, she simply sat in a wheelchair.

She moved from the hospital into a nursing home just before Mother's Day, 1999. My sister, Sue, and I had timed our visit to help Mom adjust to the new routine. The day before, a tornado ripped through their region, flattening a small town. As the plane circled before landing, I saw what looked like light-grey confetti scattered across a red carpet. The confetti turned out to be metal and wood, pieces of a house that were now strewn across the raw, orange-red clay soil.

At the nursing home, Sue pulled our rental car into a parking spot and turned the key in the ignition. We didn't move. The late afternoon sun turned the humid air in the car into a sauna.

"Okay," I said more cheerfully than I felt, then bit my lip.

"We can do this," she said.

"Yes." I took a deep breath and let it out slowly. Silently, I repeated *We can do this, we can do this* as we reeled up and down halls where strong antiseptic couldn't quite cover the smell of human waste and fear. Televisions blared from some rooms; in others, residents moaned. Still others were silent and dark, the blinds drawn, the lumps under the sheets immobile.

Bewildered, we questioned everyone wearing scrubs until we pieced together the routine of bathing, clothing, hairdressing, feeding, exercising, laundering. Meanwhile, my mother sat in a wheelchair in her room, chin in hand.

Oh, the guilt at leaving her there, yet the relief that evening as Sue and my father and I shared a quiet meal at a restaurant. No more public wrangling of my mother's confusion and incoherent insistence for attention. No more makeshift dinners at home, one sister distracting Mom while the other foraged with my father. No more wakefulness, wondering if she was sneaking out of the house in a wandering fit. We let the professionals do the difficult parts of care for yet another version of *Mom Now*.

The biggest dangers in the walk through the nightmarish swamp were behind me. Gently, the extra tension between my father and me dissipated. The journey – ours, hers – wasn't over, but we could continue as a united family.

My first day back at the office, a co-worker asked whether my parents lived near the path of the tornado. "Did you see much destruction?" she said.

I thought of the woman I'd left frowning at a catalogue, trying to pick the printed flowers from the page. *Destruction. Devastation.* "Yes," I said.

ONE WARM JUNE evening, I sat in a restaurant near my home, listening intently to the sixty-something bearded man across the table.

"Now, your mother was something else in the classroom," Dr. Durand said, his Louisiana roots making two syllables of "else." "She was as like to say, 'That's the most ridiculous thing I ever heard,' when somebody proposed a proof. And then when they'd work it out on the chalkboard, you know, she'd say, 'Well, I was wrong.'"

William Durand was my mother's first EdD advisee in mathematics in the 1960s. We had met at math department picnics when he was a graduate student and I was a child. Now he was a magician, conjuring a woman I once knew.

"She was hard," he said, looking into the past above my head. "She was a *hard* teacher, but if you did your homework, you were okay." He paused. "If you didn't, well, she'd keep calling on you till you were embarrassed enough to get it done the next time. She was...*respected*. Yes, people respected her. Students. Teachers."

The clattering dishes and conversations around me disappeared as I drank in a vaguely familiar foreign language: imaginary numbers, real analysis, topology, p-adic integers, functions, complex variables, number theory, linear algebra. These words from my mother's vocabulary swirled in beautiful patterns in front of me, whispering of a time in the distant past, when grownups were the ones who worried and I read fairy tales.

I was not a mathematician and would never fully understand of all of them, but two words glistened with new meaning: *Finite. Infinite.*

Just before we left the restaurant, he said, "Now, remember. Your mother touched the lives of so many people. She really made a difference."

Touching lives. I remembered seeing her hands covered in chalk dust after solving problems at the blackboard. Now she sat in a wheelchair with God-knows-what crusted brown under her fingernails.

For this gift from Dr. Durand, I forced my trembling lips into a smile. "Thank you."

MY MOTHER DIED from a bout of pneumonia just before midnight on May 7, 2000, a year after entering the nursing home. We had authorized an autopsy so that my mother could contribute to the knowledge base – so that she could continue to make a difference. Her brain showed changes consistent with Alzheimer's. *Probable* became *definite*.

After my mother died, I gave myself a break from learning about Alzheimer's. I wanted a *finite* experience of the disease.

But I kept learning in other areas – notably, about *love*. My mother's death brought me closer to my father. However much I missed her, I knew he missed her more. As he aged, I learned about his *chronic obstructive pulmonary disease* (COPD). He fought fungal and bacterial infections. This time, I was more prepared to be of service. I arranged to have meals delivered to his house. We spoke frankly of his will. I stayed with him often. In the last month of his life, I learned about *macrolide antibiotics* and *drug interactions*. I stood ready to move in with him, should he need it.

He didn't. And when he died, I learned that losing a parent could be simply *sad* instead of *dismal*.

But Alzheimer's disease is still there. Perhaps it's not only *out there* but also *in here,* quietly growing in my own brain. Our family has escaped the disease's known genetic markers, but we're still at increased risk. Mom's mother also showed signs of senile dementia, though it was *hardening of the arteries* in the 1950s.

And of course, I still see Alzheimer's in the news. On the cover of the January/February 2011 of *Discover*, a line trumpeted "Medicine: Alzheimer's Cure." I grabbed the magazine from the dining room table and flipped through the pages, scanning madly. Finally, the story: "Early Diagnosis for Alzheimer's."

Early diagnosis.

Oh.

Almost fourteen years after reading my mother's Christmas card, I slumped into a chair at a different kitchen table to read. Two new tools make it possible for doctors to diagnose Alzheimer's with 90 percent or greater accuracy.

Important results, yes.

But not a *cure*.

That's the word I'm still waiting to see, the book I'm still waiting to read.

Canadian Caped Crusaders

AARON BROVERMAN

USUALLY ACTIVITY MOVES through Vancouver's Charleston Park like a blood stream, but not today. Today everyone has stopped to stare at a man dressed in all black wearing a trenchcoat, a fedora, and a green skull mask sewn into a goofy Jack-o-lantern grin. He hands trading cards with his hooded face on them to children, then makes jovial small talk with a portly middle-aged English woman who has been staring at him for a while.

"How do you do?"

"Hello."

"Lovely day, isn't it?"

"It is, it's lovely." She starts to walk away, but just can't: "I think you've got Halloween slightly mixed up."

The man in the mask tells her he's always dressed like this. He doesn't tell her why, but does offer a good-natured joke: "You should see my Christmas tree."

For the homeless of Vancouver's Downtown Eastside, however, no explanation is needed. The masked man is not some kook in an out-of-season Halloween costume. He's Thanatos, The Dark Avenger. Though his name means death, those who see him recall a bringer of life: On an average night, Thanatos distributes between 10–15 basic care packages to the area's homeless, each bag packed full of necessities, including food, water, toiletries, and winter clothing. South American refugees who meet him on patrols, after their on-foot trek from Chile to Vancouver, all in search of a better life, call him Padre de Morte – "Father Death" – and venerate him as a saint. He's seen men weep when he hands them a loaf of bread. Others say seeing him during the wee hours of the morning is like staring death in the face, and that it's scared them off drugs for good. To all of them, he's exactly what he looks like: a superhero. The only rational response to a world gone nuts.

EVERY SUPERHERO HAS an origin story. In 2005, Thanatos was still a mild-mannered groundskeeper, who managed a number of buildings along Hastings Street. But he kept seeing something that bothered him deeply: people were dying in the laneways surrounding the buildings. He tried to join a number of charitable organizations, but none were a good fit. He had come to feel the organizations were motivated by funding – at the very least, they were more interested in treating the symptoms of poverty rather than curing the problem. "Nobody wanted to listen and nobody cared," he says. "I was just a guy trying to do some good and people would just say, 'Oh, that's nice of you.'"

He also found he couldn't make the personal connections he felt were important to ongoing aid. Dressed in street clothes, he was just another Good Samaritan handing out care packages. People who saw him in the morning would forget who he was by the afternoon. During this time, he still believed one man could make a difference, but he wasn't sure how. It finally came to him in 2007. A police officer told him that the Downtown Eastside's homeless had nothing to live for other than death. The statement shook him. He thought: "If that's the case, than death is going to have to start going out and taking care of these people."

At first, the 65-year-old thought about donning a robe and a scythe to call attention to those dying on the streets every day, but then, as he says, his geekiness took over. First, he took his name from the Greek God of death. Then, he built a costume inspired by his favourite pulp heroes: a long black trench coat from *The Shadow*, a matching black fedora from *The Spirit*, a cloth full face mask like in *The Green Hornet*. He wasn't interested in becoming a vigilante. Instead, he felt people in the Downtown Eastside needed help, whether it was small, intangible things, like knowing they've got someone they could talk to, or material, tangible objects to get them through the day, like clean socks or something to keep their hands warm. As Thanatos, he would be memorable and, he felt, be better able to build trust. More than anything else, he thought the mask would draw more attention to the plight of the homeless and drug-addicted in Canada's worst neighbourhood.

"If this was an ego trip, I'd be talking as myself," he says. "Instead, I can't get the press, I can't get the world's notice, as myself. I have to put on a mask to get the world's attention." Not much is known about the man behind the mask. Thanatos likes it that way. He has a wife and daughter, and under no circumstances will he let his potentially dangerous work follow him home. His wife often acts as his spotter, though, driving a safe distance behind while he's on patrol. He also wears body armour.

What we do know is that he was a Christian-raised military brat in the southern U.S. He enlisted in the Vietnam War in 1966 before being honourably discharged a decorated soldier five years later. He was briefly a police officer in

Rhodesia before spending a year in Europe and finally following his mother to Canada in 1973. By day, he now works in the death industry – a mortician, a coroner, a funeral director, he won't reveal specifics. By night, he distributes his care packages at 3:00 a.m. when people are just getting out of the shelters and the need, he says, is greatest. Though he was in the park the day I met him, it's a rare occurrence.

If Vancouver were Gotham City, the Downtown Eastside would be Crime Alley. Statistics Canada has long deemed the neighbourhood "The Poorest Postal Code in the Country" and it has one of the largest open air illicit drug markets in North America. A 2008 report from a Vancouver Board of Trade says that the neighbourhood has twice the mortality rate of the rest of the province, seven times the rate of death due to alcohol, and 38 times the rate of death due to HIV-related diseases. There are 18,000 people living in The Downtown Eastside and 20 percent are living with a mental illness. Many of them (1,600 people in Vancouver) are homeless – they have no address, but could be living with family, squatting, or in a shelter – and 306 people live on the street.

But, arguably, anyone can do homeless outreach. Why go to the extreme of wearing a mask and creating a secret identity? For some, that answer is easy. To them, we live in a world where the 24-hour news-cycle constantly gives the impression that our society is going to hell. People like Thanatos believe the world needs heroes again – not just people, but symbols and icons we can look up to and aspire to be. It's an extreme effort to recreate the straight ahead morality of the Golden Age of Comic Books in a world that seems to have no morality at all. It's the greed of our financial institutions, the violence of the War on Terror, and the partisanship of our political system versus "This looks like a job for Superman!" It's the simplicity of good versus evil.

In Canada and around the world, this worldview has spawned an entire community that dons costumes and fights against the social ills that plague their own cities. Appropriately enough, they're called real-life superheroes and, convinced of a generally apathetic society, they're not content to stand by and watch crime and poverty take over. They're cleaning up their cities one good deed at a time. "I wear the mask because what I'm doing is more important than who I am," says Thanatos. "It doesn't matter who is under this mask."

THIS REAL-LIFE JUSTICE League is hundreds of people strong. In Canada, those with a costume and a cause are a diverse bunch. There's Polarman in Nunavut, a thirty-something who's focused on child welfare and eradicating bullying for 18 years; Black Hat in Ottawa raises awareness for lyme disease; Ark Guard patrols the streets of Toronto with an eye out for suspicious activity; and Aurora, one of Canada's only active female real-life superheroes, provides communication and logistical support for her husband, Windsor's Crimson Canuck, while he's out on patrol doing homeless outreach. There's also Paladin who stops crimes in Calgary, Anonyman, who monitors gang activity in Saskatchewan, and a few others, like Sustainable Energy Man, who advocates the use of sustainable energy.

"In my mind, they're marketing good deeds," says Peter Tangen, creator of The Real-Life Superhero Project and a consulting producer on the HBO documentary *Superheroes*. "They're using the symbolism of something that is good to capture the imagination of people who witness them and people who write about them." Like Thanatos, most Canadian superheroes eschew vigilantism: They prefer outreach to crime-fighting, modesty to flamboyance, and peacekeeping to confrontation. In the U.S., where the real-life superhero movement is most popular, there are multiple heroes for every state and major city. While outreach is a component of patrols in the U.S., many blame the higher crime rates for making actual crime-fighting more common.

Such tactics don't always end heroically. One New York-based real-life superhero team, for instance, was caught on tape baiting people into committing crimes, while another real-life superhero out of Seattle was arrested and lost his job. This infamous good-deeds-gone-awry moment occurred at 2:30 a.m. on a Sunday in October 2011. That's when Seattle real-life superhero Phoenix Jones' patrol spun out of control. He and two other men spotted a brawl in the street, and Jones ran into the melee spraying mace in an attempt to break it up. "They went totally ape s--t," says Tea Krulos, a journalist who was there to research his upcoming book on real-life superheroes, *Heroes in the Night*.

"They started attacking him," adds Krulos. "This girl took off her shoe and started hitting him over and over again. They tried to run him over with a car and I even got punched in the face at one point." The police were called and Phoenix Jones was arrested. As a result, he was forced to reveal his true identity – mixed martial arts fighter Ben Fodor – and subsequently lost his job taking care of autistic children. He was later acquitted of any crime.

These types of events are rare among Canadian superheroes. "It takes a special kind of personality to put on a bat costume and avenge the death of their parents," says Joe Kilmartin, former manager of Toronto's Comic Book Lounge & Gallery. "The idea of one person going off half-cocked and taking matters into his own hands with someone who could be wielding a gun doesn't smell Canadian." Plus, it's not very legal. Expanded in 2012, Canada's Citizen's Arrest

Laws state that you can make an arrest within a reasonable length of time after a crime has been committed. Still, the arrest is only legal if it's not feasible for the police to execute and you behave in a reasonable manner, as determined by the courts. Every good real-life superhero knows this, especially Calgary's Paladin.

Calgary is actually one of Canada's safest cities. Its general crime rate has nose-dived and its homicide rate remains stable, even though it has risen in the rest of the country over the past three years. But that doesn't mean nothing happens there. Like Phoenix Jones, Paladin admits he has always had difficulty minding his own business when someone is in trouble. He's a sizeable guy, he says, fit, and has a career in security and enforcement. Plus, he also has an overabundance of "what I guess you would call chivalry." Standing by just isn't part of his natural modus operandi. Unlike Jones though, whose tactics Paladin doesn't approve of, he tries to avoid confrontation, not run towards it. "A lot of the time it's just observe and report: make sure I can pick people out, say what they're doing and relay it to the police," he says. "On average, I log four or five calls to the police per week."

There have been times, however, when he says he's been on the phone with police dispatch and has had to warn them that the situation is escalating and if the authorities don't show up soon, he will have to intervene. Once, while riding Calgary's LRT, he watched a number of men move from teasing, to bullying, to verbally assaulting another passenger for five stops. Since he was outnumbered and they hadn't moved to physical violence, he thought it wise to wait. He didn't like watching the bullying, but also thought he could help more by providing good descriptions to the police, taking pictures, and following the men discreetly. "You don't have to throw punches or try and be the big hero," he says. "You can save someone just by being there and being an active witness. You can inconvenience yourself for the sake of another person and it's actually a good feeling at the end of the day."

As a security professional in his regular life, Paladin is keenly aware of what he can do within the law and what is crossing the line. Even if Phoenix Jones was able justify using the mace under the law given the circumstances, Paladin feels de-escalation may have been a possibility – or should have, at least, been the priority. Perhaps, he muses, Jones was so intoxicated with his own image he decided to "spring into action." Paladin feels such decisions only serve to further malign real-life superheroes as volatile and inexperienced vigilantes. He's especially careful to avoid becoming the next sideshow story of the week, something he says Phoenix Jones could easily have been. Paladin never wears a costume, only extra body protection hidden underneath his civilian clothes. He's even uncomfortable with the term "Real-Life Superhero." He prefers "Extreme Altruist." "I don't want it to be about the spectacle and the violence," he says. "It's too easy for people to fixate on things like that."

WINDSOR, ONT.'S CRIMSON Canuck is bringing more heroes in his province together. In November 2011, he founded The Trillium Guards of Ontario with Ottawa's Black Hat and Toronto's Ark Guard. So far, they have least two heroes protecting every city in the province, for a total of 17 members, Ontario's very own Avengers team. "Our main goal is just to inspire other Canadians, especially young Canadians, to take an active role in their communities," says Canuck, "and [to] realize that you might hate the place that you live, but you can also work to improve it."

The Crimson Canuck started his road to real-life super-herodom two years ago after watching the *Superheroes* HBO documentary and reading an article about Thanatos. The film blew his mind. The birth of his daughter also helped shake his apathy. For the first time ever, he cared about the 38,000 people living below the poverty line in Windsor. It was time to make up for all his years of doing nothing. He didn't wear a costume in the beginning, but the former military brat (who also served as a reservist for three years) soon came to see purpose in having a uniform – it magnifies the sense of duty and obligation. In June 2012, after 10 months patrolling, he donned his maple-leaf-themed costume and now wears it on every patrol.

He wasn't wearing his costume one fateful night in 2011, however. He wasn't even on patrol. A friend had witnessed two men rob a convenience store, called police, and was hot on one suspect's trail when he ran into Canuck, who was on his way home from work. Duty called and Canuck joined the pursuit in progress. The chase ended when the suspects tried to hide in a parking garage; each friend blocked an exit and prevented them from leaving until the police arrived, at which point Canuck and his friend were easily able to direct police to the suspects. "This is something you can do anytime," he says. "You don't have to be a costumed community activist, a real-life superhero, or an extreme altruist to do any of these things."

Brave? Yes. A dangerous move for a rookie crime fighter? Possibly. Most real life superheroes believe there is a wrong way to do what they do, which is a big reason why Canuck says he established The Trillium Guards. As an organization, he and his superhero partners are presented as a united front, not just random individuals in costume. Besides, he adds, kids want to be Superman when they're young partly because of the cool company – they get to hang out with Batman, Wonder Woman, and the rest of the gang.

Members must take a pledge to join the Trillium Guards. The pledge, in part, requires members to volunteer their time in the pursuit of bettering their communities, be loyal to its citizens, and to the powers that govern it, unless they are corrupt. The Trillium Guards also have their own handbook, which outlines how members must conduct themselves while out in public and on patrol. One rule states that members must patrol in groups of two or more. Another states that members must call police to report suspicious activity, or crime, and must also stick around to give a statement. The number one rule: never act like a vigilante. The handbook also includes advice on when it's appropriate to keep a secret identity, what protection members are allowed to carry under the law, and how to act if confronted by police while on patrol. Relevant laws, such as citizen's arrest, are also explained.

If members don't follow the rules, they're out. Trillium wants to present itself as a professional organization and to operate alongside police as best it can – particularly important for its survival given law enforcement's own concerns. Staff Sgt. Brendan Dodd recently expressed those concerns in an article about real-life superheroes in the Windsor-Michigan area. "I don't recommend putting yourself in danger to address a crime that would best be handled by police," Dodd told *The Windsor Star* in November 2012. "We understand that people in our community have an interest in keeping people safe. But, most of the time, the best idea is to be observant and contact police about anything suspicious or any criminal activity going on."

Tangen believes the police have a justifiable concern. "The police," says Tangen, "have every reason to be concerned that someone may misunderstand what Phoenix Jones represents and adopt the methodology, but dismiss the morality." Take for example, the three teens from Chilliwack, B.C. who, in November 2011, lured suspected pedophiles into the open, filmed and berated them on camera – *To Catch a Predator*-style – and then posted the results on YouTube for all to see. Two were dressed as Batman, the other as the Flash. "They aren't real-life superheroes. They're just two kids dressed up as Batman and the Flash who didn't stop to think how dangerous it was and what they might be getting into," says Thanatos. "If the person had a gun or a knife, these kids could've been in a lot worse shape."

If police are less than pleased with the idea of people taking the law into their own hands, Brian Postlewait questions the need for masks at all. Postlewait is the executive director of Mission Possible, an organization dedicated to providing the opportunity for meaningful work (paid or not) to the homeless in Vancouver's Downtown Eastside. He acknowledges a costume inherently brings publicity, but adds that community social work is done best when it's done transparently – something that's pretty hard to do when no one knows your real name or what you look like. "A masked man is kind of a unique thing," he says. "At the end of the day, short-term solutions never promote the kind of transformative change we need in our communities."

Yet, at the core, Thanatos – Postlewait's own backyard superhero – uses the same approach as Rev. Liz Wall, the founder of Mission Possible. More than 20 years ago, she would drive up to the Downtown Eastside of Vancouver and serve sandwiches out of her station wagon. She believed it was important to truly know the homeless in the area, not as a demographic, but as people. She wanted those she helped to trust her and know that she truly cared for them. Thanatos builds relationships the same way. Week after week, he hands out bundles inscribed with the word "Friend" so the recipient knows he's there for them. Hearing this, Postlewait softens. "It's not about a gimmick," he says. "It's about inner character." He doesn't know Thanatos, he adds, so it's impossible to judge him. Perhaps he does have a heart of gold, says Postlewait. Maybe he really is in it for the long haul. Maybe, we really do need some superheroes.

How Poetry Saved My Life *by Amber Dawn*

HEATHER CROMARTY

To Write

GIVEN THE TASK of writing a lecture on women and fiction in 1928, Virginia Woolf, while searching for first-hand historical documentation of women's lives, found herself "looking about the shelves for books that were not there." "All these infinitely obscure lives remain to be recorded," she wrote in *A Room of One's Own,* and she encouraged women to begin the task. Woolf suspected that given a fighting chance, with money, education, access, and an undisturbed place in which to write, women could do the work of writing. Currently, we're certainly not lacking in documentation, and we're not lacking in examples to follow, yet there are still a multitude of stories to tell.

Woolf thought that novels "without meaning to, inevitably lie." Of her novel, *Sub Rosa,* Amber Dawn says that at the time it was "the closest I'll get to writing an autobiography." In her new book, *How Poetry Saved My Life,* Dawn has removed the obfuscating fictional and fantasy elements in a push towards a cleaner truth. Through prose and poetics she has created a more starkly personal document, saying "if comfort or credibility is to be gained by omitting parts of

myself, then I don't want comfort or credibility." Yet credibility is exactly what she advocates: "the written word can
be a faithful witness / if you're willing to show yourself."
While women now have produced a multitude of documents, Dawn knows that each new voice is full possibilities:

> *but this emptiness you've come to know is fertile*
> *soil that waits for fireweed and milk thistles,*
> *but until you, fabulist, have spoken.*

As a Vancouver prostitute in the 1990s, Amber Dawn lives in
a world less documented than reported. The spectre of the
Pickton[1] murders hangs over the narrative (see also Nancy
Lee's *Dead Girls*), and Dawn acknowledges all the stories
that never got told in the first person:

> *There was a missing women poster*
> *wrapped around a telephone pole...*
> *by 1999 all the cars cruising the kiddie stroll had*
>   *power-*
> *lock doors...*
> *Sheila Catherine Egan*
> *four years younger than I am,*
> *disappeared the previous July.*

As Woolf noted, women "are, perhaps, the most discussed
animal in the universe...Woman attracts agreeable essayists, light-fingered novelists,...men who have no apparent
qualification save that they are not women." For every Nelly
Arcan, there is a Chester Brown *Paying for It*. In a scene

---

1   Robert Pickton is used in this essay as a nationally recognizable symbol of the
    violence done to sex workers, though he is certainly not the only perpetrator
    of such.

with a violent client, Amber Dawn attempts an escape, but notices that her phone has been left behind. She needs to go back and retrieve it, lest he call her contact list. "It's not that I'm ashamed," she says, "it's just that this – pardon my language – fuckwad does not deserve the chance to tell my story. He has no right to reach the people I know and love." This idea is relatable to the whole project of *How Poetry Saved My Life*; don't let the fuckwads have your story.

A Woman Must Have Money

> *Why did men drink wine and women water? Why was one sex so prosperous and the other so poor? … And women have always been poor, not for two hundred years merely, but from the beginning of time. Women have had less intellectual freedom than the sons of Athenian slaves. Women, then, have not had a dog's chance of writing poetry.*

VIRGINIA WOOLF PROPOSED that a woman be independently wealthy to facilitate her writing, just as she was. Certainly, Woolf was not wrong to intimate that working for a living is a distraction from producing art. Most women, however, have to work. Amber Dawn's field, before becoming published author, is prostitution.

This is the one industry where women earn more than their male counterparts. Female sex workers can earn more per hour than at any other entry-level job. This gender bias, unique to the sex trade, has provided unwed women with financial security and opportunity since ancient times.

It's important to note that Dawn *appears* to have chosen this work. Of how and why she made this choice,

Dawn is purposefully less clear. *How Poetry Saved My Life* is "my attempt to tell – not confess – a selected few of my truths."

According to Woolf, in writing, "money dignifies what is frivolous if unpaid for." But in sex it is just the opposite. "The product is sexual fantasy, which differs from other products in that the buyer wants to be an uninformed consumer." The money Dawn makes – for the most part from male clients – is her living, pays her tuition, and allows her to financially assist the women she loves. Using this money in relationships with her romantic partners causes tension as they attempt to act out a butch-femme dynamic, whereas the femme Dawn should be "taken care of."

That she chose to spend her earnings (partially) on tuition makes Amber Dawn a "credible" sex worker to those outside the industry. "The admissible excuse for being a low, demoralized woman is survivor heroism. She should have a past tough enough to explain her bad choices. She must spend her earnings on education, not on drugs or so-called frivolous things." Dawn only gets to speak, to write books, to have an audience, because she is a "nice girl/such a smart girl/an exceptional girl/a girl with such potential," a white girl, a girl who exited the sex trade at an appropriate time. "I do represent something much larger"; she is the one that the world will listen to, so she has to start talking. Visibility only *begins* with sex workers like herself. Never once does Amber Dawn let you think that the narrative ends with her, and she takes every opportunity to remind the reader that her story is a beginning, a thin crack in the ice.

Ultimately: "This is not really about sex work.... This is about the labour of becoming whole and letting yourself see a wider panorama. It's about allowing yourself to listen to broader conversations – with your voice included – to visit

the places that have be made silent or small or wounded....
You are invited to do this work."

And a Room of Her Own

AMBER DAWN IS roughly my age and we're both dedicated
to an unnaturally red hair colour. I look at her face on the
cover of *How Poetry Saved My Life* and she's me, except I
chose working at a 7-11 to fund my undergraduate degree
and tiny apartment. That's not a value judgement. I got paid
very little at that job. At the time I remember thinking that
I could just start stripping so I could work fewer hours and
do more homework. I thought that all sex work took was
enough courage. That was probably an extremely naive view
of things.

I remember so well the feminism of the '90s; the *Sassy*-in-
duced feeling of possibility, the idea that photocopying
zines and yelling into megaphones in your subversive out-
fit of babydoll dresses, smeared lipstick, and Doc Martens
could get results:

> *claim the words*
> *slut*
> *survivor*
> *strong*
> *write them on your stomach in black marker and*
>   *dance*
> *in your underwear at punk rock shows*
> *get on stage get on the radio*
> *talk back to the men that whistle at you win*
>   *arguments*
> *shout into the megaphone.*

The '90s were the dawn of third-wave feminism, and with that came ideas of inclusivity and intersectionality. And yet in the '90s Amber Dawn the sex worker was still *outré*. A second-wave hangover said to sex workers that they are simply "servants of the patriarchy." What got me thinking about *How Poetry Saved My Life* in conjunction with Woolf was the idea that there was no figurative "room" for Amber Dawn and her ilk in identity politics. She had the money, but she had no space she could call her own within a movement that ostensibly should have been there to help her get it. There was slut pride, but there was no 'ho' pride. You could give it away, but you couldn't charge for it. You could like it, but you couldn't profit from it.

> *I learned the power of identity – the idea that even an uneducated woman, like myself, who hadn't read Mary Wollstonecraft or bell hooks, could be an expert on feminism simply because of her identity as a woman. Phrases like "as a woman of colour" or "as a lesbian mother" qualified every opinion in the collective. I was the "bad" sister. I wore a mini-skirt and had scraped knees in a room full of sensible pants and makeup-free faces. The collective also taught me that sex workers… are "servants of the patriarchy." I learned immediately that the phrase "as a sex worker" is not met with the same gravity as other women's qualifiers.*

Dawn tries to hyphenate her way into being within her lesbian relationships, as labels become increasingly politically important. To participate in identity politics, one needs to formulate some kind of identity. For Dawn, these qualifiers existed outside her profession in order to be recognized.

"This was our behind-the-eight-ball butch-femme. Ours was an elbow-grease, adult-children-of-alcoholics, there-ain't-no-such-thing-as-a-free-lunch butch-femme." In meetings and collectives, Dawn finds that activism skips over human stories, forgets the doing amid all the talking, and that politics are inherently inhumane. *How Poetry Saved My Life* is an attempt to carve out that room, for herself, and anyone who would come after her. "Survival may be the most radical thing I ever do."

After Paul Auster Spoke About Lightning

SARAH DE LEEUW

FILM FESTIVALS IN small northern communities are cele-
bratory. Sort of.

They fill the people who attend them – fleece- and toque-
and handknit-socks-wearing people of a very particular bent
it must be said – with a sense of being connected to something afar. Something hard to describe, something that is
city current and urbane, clean-shoed, condo, bike-courier
tall buildings public transit and dogs on leashes in parks.

Something the very opposite of sou'westers and mack-
inaws, cracked mud encrusted leather caulk boots drying
beside wood stoves and questions about where to put the
septic pond out back and should a bear be shot and how to
load the bed of a new twin turbo diesel engine Dodge Ram
4×4 with Arctic Cat snowmobiles.

That is something to celebrate.

Every second year, Terrace hosts a travelling film festival.
People in Terrace seem to think the festival is sponsored by
the British Columbia Arts Council and the Canada Council
for the Arts, both of which speak for themselves in terms of
'being from far away': ask anyone in Terrace and, for sure,
no one knows anyone who has ever worked at either of *those*
two places.

Posters with lots of white space, sans-serif fonts and quirky cute ironic images way too fandangled for most peoples' tastes get tacked up in the public library, the one restaurant in town that serves vegetarian dishes, the community announcement board above the grocery carts in both of the only two supermarkets, and – down the highway on the Kitsum Kalum Reserve – in the local Band Office.

Someone writes a letter to the editor of *The Terrace Standard* about the waste of taxpayers' money.

The young just-out-of-university high school English teacher develops a special class about censorship, freedom of speech, the arts, and the history of cinematography for her Grade 12 students. That young just-out-of-university high school English teacher is always, always, both brand new every second year and almost identical to the teacher before her; she moves up north from the city to be close to nature, realizes in the sleety long nights of her first winter that she'd like to have children, dates a trucker a logger a guide outfitter a cop a heavy-duty mechanic a fishermen a heli-ski operator. She tries to explain to him the virtues of lentils and being vegetarian. Then, sometime in mid-August in her second year in the north, a few months after she has broken down and started buying sliced turkey breast at the deli, when the mosquitoes just stop being too bad to even walk outside and you can finally read a book on the back deck of the trailer on the back forty which is one of the few homes for rent near town, she moves back down south after attending the film festival, during which she cries while sitting alone in the theatre's back row.

If, to try and stifle your sobs at one of the movies during the every-second-year film festival, you lean your head back while seated in the last row of seats in Terrace's movie theatre, which is an independent venture in case you didn't know, run by a husband and wife team who also own a logging camp up in Nisga'a Territory and an RV sales park on the edge of town and who have done pretty well for themselves over the last 35 years, the back of your head will touch gold shag carpets that run up, down, and all around the walls of The Tillicum Twin Theatres.

The logo of the theatres, by the way, is a Thunderbird totem pole carved by Mungo Martin in Victoria, which looks out across the Pacific ocean over 1500 kilometres southwest of Terrace. No one thinks this is unusual or says anything about it in Terrace because no one pays any attention to things like Thunderbirds who beat their massive wings, splitting open storm-silver skies with sheet lightning flashing from their eyes, from whom humans descended all those millions and millions of years ago when there was nothing but night and the earth was purely stone.

The shag carpets were Bill and Norma's late 20th century effort at soundproofing, golden efforts that are now crispy and disintegrating to the touch.

Bill and Norma's mid-1980s soundproofing idea means that after leaving the films that made you cry, made you dream of Ethiopian food restaurants and bookstores with Friday evening poetry readings, you have to pick bits of carpet scab from your scalp.

If you dared to put some kind of fancy hair product in your hair, let's say a nice smelling wax or sculpting gel because you dared to dream that you might meet another young teacher who might want to walk along a northern river hand in hand with you and then go home with you and make a salad with homegrown bean sprouts, the bits of gold carpet will stick to your hair, the back and top of your head, for days.

Even after a good washing, several days later you will find golden carpet scales on your pillow one morning when you wake up alone and exhausted by the size of everything around you. You might remember your fright when the rivers began to flood, full-throttle fatty and brown, tearing out entire cottonwood trees, because it seemed like those rivers were out to destroy the world.

Dolby Sound has yet to arrive in Terrace and who needs 3D anyway because most of those films come in the format we've been fine with for the last ten years. If Bill and Norma are going to change things up at The Tillicum Twin Theatres, they'd be better off getting rid of the bank of urinals in the women's washroom that no one, and I mean no one, has ever been able to explain. After all, it's not like there aren't urinals in the men's washroom too, which, ok yes, aren't exactly aligned and could be better affixed to the wall, which everyone knows about because at least one guy someone knows has had a hard time aiming, and even missed, when the kids in the race-car-driving video machines leaning against the other side of the urinal wall got really mad about not being able to go faster in their video race cars and kick-slammed the machines, hard, causing the urinals to shudder.

Still, even with the gold shag carpet and the race-car shuddering urinals, one weekend every 24 months at The Tillicum Twin Theatres in Terrace is taken up by Montreal documentaries, experimental shorts, indie flicks about snow boarders and skaters around Vancouver, films by Iranian feminists and, in the case of a film I saw when I was 17 and recall particularly well, slow moving dramas with unflattering sequences of a very thin woman in her mid-60s, fading blue shoulder blade butterfly tattoo, mounting a young man's erect cock in his university dorm.

In Terrace, the forty or so people who attend the film festival, many of them Grade 12 students revved up about freedom of speech and thinking about university even though their parents tell them it is not worth the price of admission and it's a helluvalot smarter to meet the foreman of CN Rail or the manager at the local sawmill, all experience these movies together. We all lean forward together. For the 16 or so hours of a dust-specked flickering funnel of light and the snap-snap-snap of reels ending, those of us attending the eight films that arrived by bus from Prince Rupert and are sometimes late because of mud and debris slides, hold our breath. Together. And exhale. Together.

Together for the hours of those films we give up the long strong light of late summer evenings that sustains us in the winter and we give up the first runs of coho and the possibility of picking pine mushrooms and we give up the most purple of purples in the world, in the shape of fireweed flowers before they turn to seed and pollen, ash white on the wind bringing in fall, and we are transported, connected to something afar.

It is much the same in Prince George.

Yes, Prince George is 573 kilometres east from Terrace along Highway 16 and, yes, Prince George has a film festival not every second year but instead for three full days every single winter and then one alternative film is screened at the local college every week during the autumn. Yes, in that way Prince George is far away from Terrace: it's a city with a Costco and a Winners and more than one high school and a university and a movie theatre with six screens, all of which play digital and have 3D options.

Still, Prince George is a northern city, a city circled by gravel logging roads punched through wilderness fast and hard to make way for clear-cutting and hauling away the dead wood from millions of hectares of pine-beetle-killed-forests. It is a city chock-a-block full of women who, in the winter when it is −30 or sometimes colder, are forced to go to work in skirts and fake-fur lined rubber boots because otherwise their feet would freeze when they shovel the driveway in the morning, their husbands away in camp or out on a rig somewhere, hands winter chapped and sometimes even bleeding from grabbing chains slick with bitumen or natural gas.

The same year that a Canadian film was nominated for an Oscar, which was a big deal even though Canadians were bitter that the nomination was in the category of Best Foreign Language Film, which seemed crazy to most of us who live in bilingual Canada but speak only English and who for the most part live within 200 kilometres of the United States border, the film festival in Prince George screened a documentary about people struck by lightning.

Act of God is a quiet film, at odds with the topic it contemplates. A group of mothers stand on the yellow-red ground of a small desert village in Mexico and look toward the moon, toward the stars, forgiving the sky for having released an evening lightning bolt that sizzled down along a metal rooftop cross and through the adobe ceiling of their town's tiny church, killing a number of their children.

The New York City author Paul Auster, whose books are among my all-time favourites and whose thin text *Why Write*, with a lightning bolt ripped across its cover, is one I have returned to hundreds of times for clarity on a question that often plagues me, speaks very softly in the film about a night that changed his life forever.

On a summer evening in 1961, Paul Auster and a group of fellow early-teen boys at a summer camp in rural New York State were led off by a group counsellor eager to expose the city boys to some real and authentic nature. In 1961, Paul Auster was of course still very young and so was very different from the man in the film who (so I had read) by then had a son who'd gone to prison and who had taken up writing novels about improbable things like doing nothing but moving stones for years on end. In the story in the movie *Act of God* that Paul Auster narrates, the cluster of boys began walking through rolling farmers' fields toward a thin line of forest on the horizon. Clouds above the boys boiled and the light slowly transformed into that awful bruised tint of pewter that people for the most part know means that a storm is getting ready, really good and ready.

In the movie, Paul Auster tells the story of that night very slowly and very matter-of-factly.

It begins to rain.

The boys are soaked.

The storm begins in earnest.

The sky is full of sheet lightning.

The lightning is splintering blinding blue terrible and everywhere.

The boys turn around and head back for camp, confused with the fury of the world unleashed all around them. They come across a fence they didn't remember crossing earlier. They form a line and one boy hoists up the bottom line of barbwire so the other boys, slick with mud and rain by now, can shimmy under. All the boys make it under and then it's the turn of the last boy, the one who held the barbwire up for everyone else, including Paul Auster.

As the last boy begins to gingerly slide under the fence, a bolt of lightning reaches down and electrifies the fence, lighting up the metal into thin sparking bands of vibrating blue heat.

I remember how quietly Paul Auster spoke about that bolt of lightning. How measured he appeared when he spoke about the bolt of lightning that shot down and through his friend, killing the boy instantly.

I think about lightning being a reason to write.

When I leave the Prince George theatre where the three-day movie festival is always screened, the night is bright and calm. There is not even an idea of lightning. Fresh snow has fallen sometime during an early film earlier in the day. The moon, while not quite a complete orb, is certainly big, a sliver or two off full. Stars sparkle and my boots squeak on the icy pavement as I walk toward my car. Still, visions of lightning shoot through my eyes when I close them, inhaling the cold winter air. I can still hear Paul Auster's voice in my head. I get into my car and pull out of the parking lot and I make a right-hand turn onto the highway that runs past one of Prince George's many grocery stores and I think about how I still live close to nature but also in a big city, comparatively speaking, and I think about movie festivals that I attended when I was much, much, younger, and I then for a moment I think about Terrace.

I remember clearly this is what I was thinking about because, the very second that I think about Terrace, a pearly white Cadillac suv streaks past me, a flash of white going at least triple my speed. I watch its bright speeding tail-lights rush towards a four-way intersection just up ahead, an intersection where I'd subconsciously noted the lights just turning red. The Cadillac does not stop. It plows front first into a small Toyota, the same year and make as the Toyota I am driving home from a documentary film while thinking about lightning and thinking about the theatre in Terrace.

I am the first person to arrive at the intersection. The small Toyota, crumpled on impact and spun several times around in the intersection before smashing into a power pole on the edge of the highway, is steaming. Steaming. All around, glass sparkles on the ice and snow that dust the highway. Despite smashing into another car, the suv has made it well through the intersection and has stopped several metres past the traffic lights, the traffic lights that are still going through their yellow-red-green sequence, oblivious to the carnage below them. I stop in the middle of the intersection under those lights, jumping out of my car and running towards the driver's side of the struck car.

Lights are popping behind my eyes, a combination of shock and seeing bright sparks that lit up the night when metal chewed into and skidded against other metal. As I reach the struck and crumpled car, a young woman with long blond hair struggles to get out of the drivers' seat, her feet crunching on glass. I hear a dog barking, a sharp high-pitched abnormal yipping as brittle as the light on glass on ice on pavement we are moving on. The woman slips, stumbling for a split second. I try to catch her while at the same time reaching to open the passenger's door behind the driver's seat. A white plastic baby car seat is buckled down in the back seat. A box of Cheerios has exploded, little "Os" littering surfaces of slowly deflating airbags. A carton of milk is ripped open, pouring over a head of lettuce that landed behind the front passenger seat. Nothing is moving in the baby seat, a pastel flowered flannel blanket tucked snuggly in around the shape of a tiny human, face invisible, everything quiet save for the bark of a dog I now see is in the far back of the car.

For a moment I have no idea what to do.

The young woman is calling from behind me 'is she ok is she ok is she ok' and the question seems in perfect rhythm with the bark of the dog and the turning of the traffic lights and the sputtering steam of the car and my breath and my heart and my breath again and I am bending into the car unbuckling the baby seat, gently manoeuvring out a plastic bucket that is shaped like a cupped hand. As I turn away from the shadow of the wrecked car, light settles upon the flannel blanket and everything is glinting inside the baby seat, shards of glass coating the pink flowered flannel blanket, resting on silence. I set the baby seat on the pavement and in the distance I hear sirens and the woman is still calling 'is she ok is she ok is she ok is she ok,' this time closer, right next to me, beside me, and I see my hands and I see the hands of the mother and we are reaching into the white plastic cupped hand and slowly peeling back the flannel blanket, the sound of bits of glass dropping onto ice on pavement and then there is the face of a baby.

And then that baby screams.

Oh she screams.

The dog stops barking.

The young woman is sobbing, sobbing, gingerly lifting the baby from the car seat, crouching with baby pressed into chest and then sitting on the edge of the highway median beside her steaming car.

I walk around to the back of the car and open the hatchback and I take the dog by his collar and I lead him to his owner and then we are all sitting. The dog is shaking. Shuddering really. His whole body. I hold onto his collar with my left hand and with my right hand I rub the woman's back, circles circles circles as the sirens approach, bright blue lights. The baby is still screaming. I look at my feet and notice a smear of coagulating blood the toe of my boot. I have no idea where it came from. I have not noticed any bleeding. I think about cameras, panning slowly, shooting all the films I have seen in my life. I recall walking out of a darkened theatre into a darkening summer evening when I was a teenager in Terrace, the stationary outstretched wings of a Thunderbird above me, somewhere a storm, somewhere a northern river in summer flood, the winter snow pack melting far away in mountain valleys I have still not seen.

Boy Next Door: Growing Up in the Shadow of Paul Bernardo

STACEY MAY FOWLES

IT'S A MAY evening in 1990, and I am eleven years old, heading to gymnastics class at the high school across the street from my home in Scarborough, a suburb east of Toronto. I'm tall for my age but a slight thing, in a tie-dyed T-shirt and jean cut-offs, white-blond hair clipped back in pink barrettes. I'm a late bloomer, eagerly waiting for my body to develop into something else. Something *wanted*.

I'm allowed to walk by myself in the early spring evenings when it's still light outside. My mother watches from the window and waves, smiling (something she still does today, more than twenty years later, when I leave her house after a visit). At eleven, I don't notice the concern on her face as I walk down the driveway past our beige Volvo, across the street, and through the school parking lot. She keeps an eye on me until I enter the building.

(Many years later, I ask her how she felt about me running ahead or going out alone, given the climate of the time. "I was terrified," she says. "But I wanted you to be free.")

Once inside, I pass the administrative offices, the auditorium, and the glassed-in library, and make my way through the fluorescent-lit hallways to the gymnasium. There are kids everywhere, their parents trying to wrangle them amid the chaos. The gym is arranged with all sorts of equipment, and I'm eager to walk the balance beam and jump the pommel horse.

What's important in my memory of that night is the bulletin board at the entrance of the gym and the police sketch pinned to it. The image is of a man's face, made with a computer when computers were still rare. His expression is impassive, betraying nothing. I haven't seen his picture before, but it has just appeared on the front page of the *Toronto Star*.

When I ask my instructor who he is, she tells me that he is the man everyone has been looking for, the bad man who has been hurting women. Next to the photo, a statement reads:

> "[*Male, white*] *18–22 years, 5′10–6′, med muscular build, clean shaven, tan complexion, light coloured eyes, possibly blue, blond hair parted on left side, hair feathered just over top of right ear. Clothing: baby blue nylon hip-length jacket, tan coloured knee-length walking shorts with pleated front, running shoes, no socks.*"

I know little about sex beyond the schoolyard conjecture spread by girls with older siblings. We discuss what boys will do to our bodies, the pleasure that may come from that. We brag about the scrambled porn we've seen late at night on the television, while our parents sleep. We rub our bodies together with mocking, blushing glee. We wrap Ken's and Barbie's smooth limbs around each other's plastic torsos. We are on the cusp of knowledge, misinformed yet sure of ourselves.

But we do know about rape. Every child in my neighbourhood knows about rape, because it is everywhere and has been for years. It lurks at bus stops and calls from headlines, whispers its way into half-understood playground conversations, screams from the six o'clock news as my parents usher me away from the TV set in the rec room. For three years, a man, known only as the Scarborough Rapist, has been stalking and assaulting young women. He has been following them from bus stops, attacking them brazenly in public spaces. The neighbourhood marinates in its own fear and paranoia, and hungrily consumes the media-driven suspicion and helplessness.

The mystery man looks like the idols in my pop music magazines, handsome and baby faced. When the image was released, there were written descriptions from the victims, media reports likening him to the boy next door, but somehow we still expected him to look like a menacing villain.

After my gymnastics class, I head toward the main entrance of the school and pass a dozen photographs of graduating classes, each year hung sequentially in a long row. The students wear identical black robes, and they stare at me, hundreds of hopeful teenagers saying goodbye. Among them is a far more accurate image of the Scarborough Rapist than the sketch on the bulletin board. A tiny portrait of Paul Bernardo. Class of 1982. Head cocked, beaming grin.

I WAS RAISED in Guildwood Village, a pretty, tree-lined community at the eastern end of Scarborough. A suburb within a suburb, it sits snugly between Greyabbey Trail in the east and the end of picturesque Sylvan Avenue in the west. People leave their doors unlocked, and kids play on lawns and in the streets well into the evening. Where the neighbourhood connects with busy six-lane Kingston Road, a strip of indistinguishable mini-malls, sports bars, and no-tell motels, it feels like those no man's lands on ancient maps: "Beyond this place, there be dragons."

At the southern edge of Guildwood lie the Scarborough Bluffs, a majestic escarpment alongside Lake Ontario that invites daytime joggers and dog walkers, nighttime lovers and "bluff parties" – local slang for teenage beer-and-bonfire mischief. Lining the bluffs is a forest, conveniently accessed from Sir Wilfrid Laurier Collegiate Institute by a hole (now sealed) cut in the towering chain-link fence. Teenagers regularly snuck into the woods to smoke joints, drink, and make out.

Reported attacks by the Scarborough Rapist began in 1987. In May that year, a twenty-one-year-old woman was assaulted and beaten close to her parents' house by a man who had followed her after they both got off the same bus. Fourteen incidents in Scarborough, the last one in 1990, were known by the police well before Bernardo's ultimate conviction in 1995 for the murders of Leslie Mahaffy and Kristen French, teenage girls that he and his wife, Karla Homolka, abducted, raped, and murdered in their St. Catharines home in 1991 and 1992.

Around the same time that the computer image was released, I recall our health teacher taking the female students aside for a series of mandatory sex education classes. While we sat uncomfortably at our desks, she showed us cryptic anatomical line drawings of male and female body parts on the overhead projector, stoically demonstrated how to unroll a condom over a five-inch wooden shaft, and encouraged us to write anonymous questions on tiny scraps of notebook paper, which she answered in a monotone from the front of the class. Then, after providing the mechanics, she warned us that our bodies held something valuable that was waiting to be ruined.

"Men and boys will try to take sex from you," I remember her saying. "You have to fight them off as hard as you can."

News of the Scarborough Rapist was ever present, and the spectre of violence consumed our daily lives. Our parents warned us not to go into the woods, but my friends and I did anyway. We jumped out from behind trees to scare each other, the sound of our screams and laughter echoing through the woods like a wolf call tempting the very devil we had been taught to avoid. We were like children in wartime; danger lurked everywhere, but we had no choice but to play. We had no choice but to learn how our bodies worked at the same moment as we were told to hide them away. We had no choice but to grow up.

In the summers of our early adolescence, we rode our bikes through the endless cul-de-sacs, filling the day to get to night. When it finally came, we would collect bottles of cider and cans of Molson Canadian; we would roll joints on coming-of-age novels and slot them carefully into packs of du Maurier cigarettes. We would make out with boys in the wet summer grass, always aware that the monster waited somewhere in the distance.

ON A SUMMER day in 2011, I sit on the curb across the street from Bernardo's childhood home in Guildwood. It's less than two kilometres from the house I grew up in, located on a handsome street – one on which Bernardo reportedly admitted to committing a sexual assault in March of 1986. Unlike the other homes on the block, there is no cheerful garden, no stately tree on the lawn, just a bland brick box on a plot of land, the drapes closed tight, the carport empty. Bernardo's parents, Ken and Marilyn, still live there.

Twenty years after the reign of the Scarborough Rapist, I had returned to find out what happens when children grow up, as my friends and I did, in the murky depths of a community's fear. I had known the basics of Bernardo's crimes, but as a little girl I was shielded by my parents from the dark details, and as an adult I had chosen to avert my gaze. That summer, though, I had begun to delve into the record of his offences: hundreds of newspaper accounts, documentaries, and true crime books. The story had captured international attention for years. The public was fixated on the lurid crimes, his "Ken and Barbie" marriage to Homolka, their rape and murder of her younger sister Tammy, and the videotaped torture and murders of Mahaffy and French. The graphic, exhaustive media accounts were unsettling and controversial, and in 1993 a publication ban was imposed on Homolka's preliminary inquiry, with the judge citing Bernardo's right to a fair trial.

In 1995, the *Star* reported that calls to rape crisis centres and helplines increased by 30 percent in the period leading up to Bernardo's conviction. Gail Robinson, director of the women's mental health program at Toronto General Hospital, said she had treated a number of patients with post-traumatic stress disorder, exacerbated by the relentless coverage. The high-profile case has followers even now. Internet forums such as Watching True Crime Stories and Darker in the Light post pictures of Bernardo in his prison cell and offer updates on Homolka's life since her release in 2005. As recently as August 2013, Bernardo's face appeared on the cover of the *Toronto Sun*, his application to be transferred to a medium-security prison becoming front page news.

When I found myself on the curb across from the Bernardo home, I already knew the details of his crimes and his disturbing upbringing. His father was a peeping Tom who molested Paul's sister, and his verbally abusive mother lived almost exclusively in the basement. His father was physically abusive and called his wife a "bitch" and a "big fat cow." Paul adopted these sorts of insults for her when he discovered, at the age of sixteen, that he was the biological child of a man she had had an affair with. He would later call his victims similar names during his attacks.

As the Scarborough Rapist, Bernardo committed unspeakably vicious assaults: he raped women orally, vaginally, and anally, often cutting and penetrating them with a knife. He choked them and punched them in the face. He would later brag about his crimes to Homolka, and then with her help he intensified his attacks to kidnapping and murder.

According to media reports, after Bernardo's arrest a police officer assigned to prepare the official transcript of the footage of French's and Mahaffy's torture collapsed, weeping, and couldn't continue. I had a similar reaction while reading it. The smallest details haunted me: during one prolonged assault, Bernardo took a break to rent a movie and grab a pizza, and another time Homolka cooked a chicken dinner for the couple and their victim.

The real terror was that it felt so ordinary and suburban, that the vilest acts occurred in the spaces we thought were safe. I was struck by the same sense of banality, looking at the home where Bernardo grew up.

Evil was not foreign to our idyllic community. It had been with us all along.

IN FEBRUARY 1993, just after Bernardo's arrest on a combination of charges relating to the Scarborough rapes and the two murders in St. Catharines, the *Star* ran multiple stories about the evolving case. Among the other details, the paper revealed that ten years earlier Bernardo had graduated from Sir Wilfrid Laurier Collegiate Institute. Six months after his arrest, I started grade nine at the same school. Nicknamed "last-chance Laurier," it used a semester system that enabled students failing at other schools to collect the credits necessary to graduate as soon as possible.

Some of the roughest teenagers from across Scarborough commuted in for the program. While I was at Laurier, I witnessed or heard accounts of the following: girls drinking vodka and orange juice in the bathroom, kids sharing joints in the smoking area, skinheads gathering around the flagpole on the front lawn. One student had his teeth bashed in with a combination lock; another was cut around his eye with a broken bottle, and still another got slashed with a machete. The beatings and fights were too numerous to count. At Laurier, survival depended on the ability to remain under the radar, to never attract attention. Barring the occasional torment from mean girls, I mostly succeeded.

In grade nine, I was a cheerleader for the Laurier Blue Devils, Bernardo's former football team. The twelve-girl squad, in our white and navy uniforms, performed on the sidelines in the chill autumn rain, hoping the players on the field would notice us. That year, I developed a crush on a loud boy with a stocky build who was much older than me. I had never really been touched by a boy and had only been kissed a handful of times, yet I fantasized about his big, thick hands on me.

One day, he approached while I was sitting on the hall floor with my back against my locker. He stood above me, smiling. "I thought maybe we could go to the pond in Rouge Park," I remember him saying, naming a quiet, secluded spot where teenagers liked to park. "It's nice there at night."

AS THE SCARBOROUGH Rapist's confidence grew, the violence of his assaults escalated. He stole one victim's ID, noted her home address, and threatened to kill her family. He broke another victim's arm, and stabbed others. The police created a special task force, set up surveillance, and increased their patrols in the Guildwood area. Public forums on sexual assault were held at local high schools, where women were told to protect themselves, particularly when travelling by public transit at night. With the assistance of the FBI, the police constructed a profile of the assailant, and some sixty law enforcement agents from Canada and the United States worked on the case.

There remained a sense, however, that these efforts were inadequate. When a nineteen-year-old student was raped in April 1988 after exiting a bus, Lois Sweet wrote in the *Star* that the young woman "is now suffering from the physical and emotional aftermath of Monday night's prolonged, vicious attack. But eventually she will also have to cope with the knowledge that her community allowed it to happen." The woman had been attacked between two houses, below a bedroom window, and her screams for help were heard but ignored.

Sometimes, women themselves were blamed for the rapes. "Don't expect people to watch out for you if you happen to come back at 1 a.m. in the morning off the bus," Constable Vic Clarke told the press in June 1988, after several women who had been attacked came forward in Scarborough. "It would be nice to think that you can go anywhere you like nowadays, but don't put yourself in a vulnerable position." That same month, Alderman John Mackie proposed a curfew for women.

In response to the assaults, the Toronto Transit Commission instituted its Request Stop program. In the evening, women could ask bus drivers to drop them off between stops, closer to their destination. "I was truly freaked out," a woman who lived in Scarborough back then told me. "I was waiting for a bus, and a man walking past said, 'You should be careful. I could be the Scarborough Rapist.' I waited until he was out of sight and speed-walked to the nearest restaurant. I called my parents for a ride."

In October 1988, the media reported that a woman had managed to escape an attack, but not without receiving multiple stab wounds to the thighs and buttocks. Bernardo used his own knife, but women were subsequently warned not to carry a weapon for protection because the rapist might use it against them.

It was a victim in May 1990 who put a face to the Scarborough Rapist, and her description of Bernardo led to the sketch I saw on the gymnasium bulletin board. It ran in newspapers with the headline "Is this 'boy-next-door' the Scarborough rapist?" and 16,000 tips were given to the police that summer. In all, they received 41,000 tips from the public.

After the image ran, a woman who worked with Bernardo brought it to the office and joked about the similarity. Another employee contacted the police about the likeness, but they didn't pursue it. They did, however, follow up on a concerned call in September 1990 from the wife of an old neighbourhood friend of Bernardo's. After interviewing Bernardo for a half-hour, they concluded that he was credible, well educated, well adjusted, and congenial. He voluntarily gave a DNA sample.

While women were warned not to be easy targets, Bernardo hid in plain sight. The police collected samples of the Scarborough Rapist's DNA from victims, but it sat untested on a shelf for years, along with samples from 224 other rape suspects. Forensic scientists were busy with what the police considered more serious murder cases.

Bernardo's DNA was not compared with the Scarborough Rapist sample for more than two years, after he had already escalated to murder.

ON THE SAME day that I sat outside Bernardo's childhood home, I paid a visit to my old high school. It was the first time I had gone there in thirteen years, and it looked run-down, with paint peeling from the walls and overhead lights flickering. In the halls, I passed clusters of summer school students. The occasional harried teacher eyed me warily but said nothing. I wandered aimlessly, not entirely sure what I was looking for.

Eventually, I headed back to the foyer, searching for the line of graduating class portraits. For almost the entire time I was a student at Laurier – long after Bernardo had been arrested – his class picture had hung there. New students would often seek it out, lightly touching the glass while staring solemnly. At a school where I had witnessed violence and misbehaviour, this was one object to which we showed deference.

In my last year of high school, I heard that a girl younger than me, a petite punk with platinum blond hair and heavy black eyeliner, had pulled down the picture from the wall. The rumour was that she carried it out of the back of the building and into the parking lot, threw it in the trunk of a car, and brought it to a party where classmates sat around it, downing beers.

I like to think it was an act of defiance, an attempt to protect us from Bernardo, to do what the police and the community had failed to do for his victims. In the foyer, I see that the space where the photo once hung remains empty. No one has made an effort to fill it, or to move the remaining portraits to disguise the vacancy.

There is just a hole where his image once smiled out at the world.

WHEN I WAS fourteen, I wrote the name of that older, stocky boy I had a crush on inside a big, looping heart in purple ink in my diary. When he asked me out to Rouge Park, I felt special and chosen. I wore a blue gingham bra with tiny pink flowers stitched on it, in the hope that he might see it.

No one was afraid of the boy, and no one warned me about him. He didn't carry a knife. He didn't steal my ID, or tell me he was going to murder my family if I told anyone about what happened. What he did to me that night never made the news.

I remember his erection in his white cotton boxer briefs. I remember how he ripped a button from my shirt when he forced it off. I remember the musky, rank smell of his thick body on top of me. I remember how cold I was, and that I wondered, strangely, where the geese go when it gets that cold.

I remember thinking that no one would believe me if I told them I hadn't wanted what he did to me. I thought I had made myself vulnerable, despite everything I had been taught about keeping myself safe. And when the boy was done with me, I was grateful that he let me go, that he drove me home, that he told me I was pretty. It is a discomforting gratitude I have carried for two decades.

WHEN YOU ARE a young woman and your body becomes a crime scene, a reminder of tragedy, how can you ever come to love it? For years, I didn't tell anyone what happened to me. I never felt there was anyone to tell or anything to be done. I believed I had to endure it. I even felt lucky that it hadn't been worse – the worse I had been cautioned about by police warnings and the evening news. I didn't learn how to protect myself. Instead, I learned how to be afraid for my entire life.

Rape has a default narrative. It is the one I grew up with in Scarborough, and it has been buoyed by television crime shows, sensationalized media reports, and the myopic way we define victims and their attackers. In this narrative, a rapist jumps from the bushes, a woman is assaulted, she presses charges, there is a conviction. What we rarely acknowledge is that most victims, and their communities, never find justice or solace, at all.

Bernardo was ultimately convicted of the first-degree murder and aggravated sexual assault of Leslie Mahaffy and Kristen French, and in 1995 was sentenced to life in prison without parole. Despite DNA evidence linking him to earlier sexual assaults, he was never convicted of the Scarborough rapes. The Crown did not see the need to pursue the additional charges.

Six years later, in 2001, after I had moved away to attend university in Montreal, an Ontario court ordered that the videos Bernardo made of his crimes be destroyed. The parents of the two girls attended the event, along with several individuals who worked the case. Together they witnessed the destruction of the videos, the crime scene photos, and other evidence. For the families, their existence had long represented a violation, and their obliteration was a relief.

During the summer I spent immersed in research about Bernardo and his crimes, I thought a great deal about the question of closure and what it means for victims, for families, for communities, for me. In our search for closure, we often fail to accept that violence alters us permanently.

I came across a story that ran in the *Star*, published soon after the trial concluded, which argued that Bernardo was not the monster we wanted to believe him to be, but rather "one of us," a product of our culture, a man groomed with a pervasive, violent hatred of women. Marilou McPhedran, a women's rights advocate, spoke of the insidious impact Bernardo had had on our community, that he had created an ambient trauma even for those who had not been directly victimized by him. It is a wound that will probably never heal.

"The Bernardo case has been played out as a titillating drama," she said, "and we've failed to understand what it's done to us."

The Assault on Science

NAOMI K. LEWIS

BY MAY 2012 morale was low throughout Canada's scientific community – and then the country's scientists received a swift kick where it counts. The Department of Fisheries and Oceans (DFO) announced that, before a year went by, they would pull funding and close the Experimental Lakes Area near Kenora, Ontario. At the University of Ottawa, Katie Gibbs, almost finished her Ph.D. in conservation biology, was already concerned the Harper government's attitude toward applied research did not bode well for her field, the raison d'être of which, she says, is to affect policy. The ELA's closure was her breaking point. At the ELA-directed for two decades by David Schindler, who went on to become the Killam Memorial Professor of Ecology at the University of Alberta – scientists experimented on entire lakes. Schindler's work there helped make the world take notice of acid rain and demonstrated the ecologically devastating effect of phosphates, leading to their ban from detergents. This unique and vital resource for environmental scientists and citizens alike cost Canadians only $2 million annually.

Gibbs, along with a few other grad students and faculty, organized a rally on Parliament Hill; they perceived the closure as the latest attack in the Harper government's war on science – specifically, on any evidence that might threaten the government's ideological and economic agendas. The "Death of Evidence" event in July 2012, at which Gibbs and her associates staged a mock funeral, complete with coffin, was not the intimate gathering they'd envisioned – some 2,000 participants showed up and national and international media took note. The rally was so successful that people kept asking Gibbs what was next. What was the next step toward resuscitating evidence from its tomb under the federal government?

After defending her dissertation, Gibbs decided to work on this issue full time, and, with some of her fellow Death of Evidence organizers, founded the national not-for-profit Evidence for Democracy, which advocates the transparent use of evidence in government decision-making. Despite its rather significant airtime, Gibbs says the assault on public science – that is, science conducted by government employees – may be difficult for the Canadian public to follow because it has played out over many years and no single incident seems terribly dire: "It's only when you put them all together and look at the full timeline of events that you see this is really a systematic attempt to stifle public science."

The current status of science and evidence in Canada is dire – and no field is more under attack than environmental science. With the country's most glaring source of tension between economy and (potential) evidence right in our midst, no one should be more concerned than Albertans.

THE "EVIDENCE FOR Democracy" website provides just the kind of full timeline Gibbs thought the public needed, highlighting key events beginning with November 2007's new Environment Canada policy requiring communications officers to mediate all media interviews with scientists.

Since then, journalists have struggled for access to public scientists, sometimes only hearing back days after a request, when the article in question has already been published. Ottawa-based Mike De Souza, who covers energy and environment for Postmedia News, says it goes without saying that accessing government scientists has become difficult under the current government. Reporters are often asked to send their questions in advance of an interview and to explain what the story will address. Any journalist understands that a good interview doesn't work that way: The answer to one question prompts further questions, and the whole conversation determines the direction of the story. Worse, a reporter's emailed questions often receive answers attributed to, but not written by, the scientist in question (and that reek of PR). Sometimes journalists don't hear back at all. De Souza was writing a story in February about groundwater contamination from the oil sands and requested an interview with a scientist from Natural Resources Canada about research under the federal and Alberta governments' Integrated Oil Sands Monitoring Program. As of the end of July, De Souza had yet to get any such scientist on the phone.

"It's a fundamental issue of our democracy," says Gibbs. "On the one hand, this is public research that we pay for through our tax dollars, so we have a right to know what that research is .... And on the other hand ... having an informed public is really the foundation of a healthy democracy, and you can't have that when this research is not getting out and when the government is tightly controlling what does get out to the public."

And tightly controlling they are. We've witnessed several high-profile cases in which scientists were prevented from speaking about the potentially devastating evidence they had demonstrated – Kristi Miller of the DFO on the decline of Fraser River sockeye salmon; David Tarasick of Environment Canada on a hole twice the size of Ontario in the ozone layer over the Arctic; not to mention Canada's public scientists being trailed by media relations officers at April 2012's Polar Year conference in Montreal – but as Gibbs says, those cases can easily appear isolated and extreme. Perhaps more disturbing, she proposes, is that even journalists working on "mundane, non-exciting things like snowfall patterns and bison genes, that are absolutely not controversial at all…are still not allowed to get access." De Souza confirms that he runs into roadblocks whenever he tries to get a scientist from any federal government department on the phone, for any story.

Given this dearth of available evidence, there's plenty of room to flood media with manipulative PR. You can tell there's a problem when government and industry increase their TV and Internet ads about a particular issue, says Bill Donahue, an environmental biologist, ecologist and lawyer who works for Edmonton non-profit Water Matters. And we're seeing an all-time high for ads touting Canada's alleged environmental stewardship, especially pertaining to the fossil-fuels industry. Natural Resources Minister Joe Oliver announced his department intends to spend $16.5-million on ads this year. The NDP says this represents a 7,000 per cent increase to Natural Resources' ad budget over 2010–2011. Such messaging may not entirely convince the public, Donahue says, but it clouds the issue, and "if we can confuse people, then they don't really understand where the truth lies. And – well, it's business. It comes down to billions of dollars, and energy. Unfortunately."

IN FEBRUARY THE Environmental Law Centre at the University of Victoria and the national non-profit Democracy Watch submitted to federal information commissioner Suzanne Legault the report *Muzzling Civil Servants: A Threat to Democracy*, along with a request to formally investigate the Harper government's silencing of federal scientists. The report consists of arguments meant to show that the federal government's communications policies are illegal because they hamper the public's rights as laid out in Canada's Access to Information Act. Legault agreed to investigate seven departments: Environment Canada, Fisheries and Oceans, Natural Resources, Defence, the National Research Council of Canada, the Canadian Food Inspection Agency and the Treasury Board Secretariat.

The Harper government has offered no defence – only denials. As Legault took on her investigation, Gary Goodyear, Minister of State for Science and Technology, informed Postmedia science reporter Margaret Munro about Environment Canada's 1,200 media interviews in the preceding year, and of the government's annual 2,000-plus scientific publications. Goodyear's director of communications, Michele-Jamali Paquette, told Munro, "We reject the accusations that we are muzzling scientists." She defended the communications policy and argued that government scientists, as civil servants, "don't own the intellectual property for their work."

Paquette did not respond to my request for an interview. I asked in the same email for a breakdown of interviews granted with federally employed scientists over the last five years – who talked to whom, about what. A few days later, I received an unsigned response from a "media relations" email address. "We understand that research findings and their benefits must be effectively communicated and shared with Canadians," the email said. "The numbers show that not only does this Government stand behind its scientists; we are making more of the data they generate available to Canadians than ever before." Such is what journalists receive when we ask for facts. *Maclean's* magazine received an almost identical response when seeking insight from Goodyear and Paquette in May.

AS FAR AS Canadian journalists and our readers are concerned, public science – evidence accrued with our tax dollars – may as well lie buried alive under the Parliament buildings. But Donahue says public scientists run into roadblocks far beyond their relations with the media; they can be held up by red tape when applying for funding to conduct their research and even when attempting to publish their research. Gibbs says the government's total budget for scientists has stayed more or less the same, but that they have eliminated many science positions in the last few years, reducing the amount of research undertaken. Meanwhile, they have shifted funds, "commercializing research that's done in Canada."

That means money is diverted away from programs such as the Experimental Lakes Area and toward "the manufacture of widgets to sell," as Schindler, now a high-profile advocate for scientific integrity, puts it. He rages against the shift from "curiosity-based" research, arguing that environmental-research programs such as the ELA save billions of dollars by circumventing large-scale environment damage. "They [the government] don't understand that some expenses [help] avoid expensive reclamation, to say nothing of societal and environmental benefits," he says.

Thomas Duck, associate professor of physics and atmospheric science at Dalhousie University, stresses that

Environment Canada exists to monitor environment conditions, give us insight into what's going on in our environment and protect the health and safety of Canadians. "By eliminating those capabilities, they are, in a very real sense, putting our health and safety at risk," he says. And Environment Canada eliminates those possibilities partly by diverting resources, as Duck experienced first-hand with his work at the Polar Environment Atmospheric Research Laboratory in Eureka, Nunavut, which was recently closed due to funding cuts. "A couple of springs ago, we saw the first-ever hole in the ozone layer over the Arctic," he says. "The government responded by shutting down the ozone research program at Environment Canada."

Duck stresses that government scientists are responsible for vital research that university-employed scientists simply cannot undertake. "It's not really fair to say that if the government can't do it, then the academic sector can," he explains. Environment Canada has a mandate for environmental protection, which requires long-term – sometimes decades-long – systematic measurements. Meanwhile an important mandate for many academics is teaching students how to be researchers, and that usually means taking on research projects of three to five years.

Once a scientist has acquired funding and undertaken her research, she is still not necessarily free to make her findings public – not through the media, and now not even in peer-reviewed journals. In February the DFO established a new policy that requires supervisors to sign off on researchers' papers after they are accepted by peer-reviewed journals – which means, of course, that the department can put the brakes on publication.

Moreover, scientists' ability to affect policy is impeded because they apparently have no influence on decision makers: When political leaders, federal and Albertan, talk about the impact of major development, Donahue says, their facts are usually wrong. This spring, for instance, Gary Goodyear defended the ELA's closure, stating that according to the latest science, we don't need whole lakes to discern the impacts of contaminants. "That is absolutely 100 per cent wrong," says Donahue. "It's the opposite of what the latest science tells us." In fact, by cutting funding to the Experimental Lakes Area, the government undermined scientists' capacity to test the impact of development-related contaminants on water. The facts may have been lost somewhere in the layers of bureaucracy between Goodyear and any actual scientist. Either that, says Donahue, or Goodyear was outright lying.

Which – either way – brings us back to the importance of media access: With so many layers of bureaucracy between scientists and the ministers they work under, the media provides the best way for scientists to communicate, even to those ministers. Change can happen when evidence of harm becomes public knowledge and politicians are forced to act, Donahue says.

OUR FEDERAL GOVERNMENT has isolated scientists from the media and thereby the public, has redirected research toward the goal of immediate profit, and has even begun creating policies with the power to prevent dissemination of information within the scientific community – and all Canadians should take notice. But, for Albertans, the tarry black elephant in the room dwells up by Fort McMurray.

With Canada's economy heavily invested in fossil-fuel development, many departments suffering muzzling and cuts are linked to the oil sands. For instance, Duck says, we've seen a major scaling back of regulations that govern where and when pipelines can be built, thanks to radical changes to the Fisheries Act, the Navigable Waters Protection Act and the Canadian Environmental Assessment Act. In fact, Duck says, on June 18, 2012, the omnibus "Budget" Bill C-38 replaced the Environmental Assessment Act outright, and the next day 3,000 environmental assessments across Canada were cancelled. About 600 of those were related to fossil-fuel development.

The Harper government's inept attempt to bolster the oil sands' international image is certainly not doing industry any favours. In general, Canada's international reputation, in terms of environmental stewardship, is tanking. Duck argues "the government of Canada has done the fossil-fuels industry in this country a tremendous disservice. Two years ago, pipelines weren't in the news. The federal government, through their reckless cuts to science and through their demolition of our environmental protections...have caused the fossil-fuel industry a world of trouble."

While the federal government is responsible for determining the environmental impacts of fossil fuel development, so too is Alberta's provincial government – specifically Alberta Environment and Sustainable Resource Development (ESRD). While the federal government has received a litany of bad press about its communications policies, our provincial government has stayed pretty well under the radar. Jessica Potter, ESRD's acting director of communications, says the department has no formal policy regarding scientists' dealings with the media; that the department encourages its scientists to speak to reporters and provides training to help those experts overcome nervousness and inaccessible, jargon-heavy explanations. Communications staff do act as spokespeople quite often, she concedes, but mostly because the experts are not as comfortable giving interviews and have other work to do. The department keeps track of interviews, she says, so they can post the answers to commonly asked questions online.

And the province does have a better reputation than the feds among journalists – though not as much among scientists, who say the province has its own methods of skirting evidence that bodes ill for the oil sands. The government of Alberta's tactics include allowing scientists Donahue identifies as "professional expert witnesses" to testify at hearings (these are scientists who make their living defending industry interests, who often haven't published in years or decades, says Donahue). Then again, some scientists say the province has pushed the federal government further toward environmental responsibility and transparent monitoring than it would have gone otherwise – although the province "needs to push harder," says Duck. "It's clear that they [the provincial government] want to get a much better handle on the environmental risks associated with the oil sands," he says. "And that makes a lot of sense, because those environmental risks will largely be borne by Albertans in the future. Albertans have a real serious vested interest in knowing what this [oil sands development] is going to do to their beautiful province."

In spring 2012, federal Minister of the Environment Peter Kent and Alberta's ESRD minister, Diana McQueen, announced the Integrated Oil Sands Monitoring Plan, a joint project between the two governments. To what extent the federal and provincial governments are true partners in this project is difficult to determine; Schindler worked on the plan, and says though Alberta Environment claims to be in the lead on the project, he hasn't seen much evidence of that in the field. In fact, he says, though Alberta Environment had one person at the table, that person did not contribute or say much. In any case, on April 22 of this year – Earth Day, of course – Kent and McQueen launched an online "Joint Data Portal," which, Kent announced, "provides the public with ongoing access to the credible scientific data collected…and the methodology used to produce it." He added, "The scope and volume of monitoring data will continue to increase through to 2015."

No one denies that the plan, and the portal, are encouraging developments. "A step in the right direction" was the phrase I heard again and again. But – there are a lot of buts. After the Alberta and federal governments announced their Integrated Oil Sands Monitoring Plan, Duck points out, they cut a number of the capabilities needed to implement it. He names ozone research, measurements by aircraft and smokestack sampling as examples. The word among scientists is that we can't know yet how useful the available information will prove.

They also point out that monitoring is not the same as actually taking action. The plan includes no guidelines for what to do should problems be discovered. Perhaps the biggest concern is the monitoring plan's lack of third-party oversight – though, according to Potter, Alberta is currently building an arms-length monitoring agency that will provide such oversight for all environmental monitoring in the province, beginning in the oil sands region, and including the joint oil sands monitoring program. The government intends to have the agency in place by the end of 2013, she says.

Schindler, for one, isn't holding his breath. The Alberta government has promised the incorporation of an independent monitoring panel three years in a row, he says, and it still hasn't happened. In his estimation, the chances of that agency ever coming together are 50/50. Donahue voices a similar skepticism. When things need to happen quickly, they do, he says; the province is dragging its feet on this one.

Furthermore, access to raw data is not particularly useful without access to the scientists who collected that data, who can explain their collection methods – nor is that raw data interpretable for most lay people, including journalists. And those scientists who could explain the data, of course, are difficult or impossible to reach, as Mike De Souza has experienced. Schindler says he hopes the portal will improve, but that it "right now seems like part of the muzzling problem" and "largely a dumping ground and another propaganda portal," mostly aimed at impressing the U.S. "And it's not working," he adds.

Why propaganda? The information portal's "Latest Data" page assures citizens that, despite the oil sands emitting contaminants, "Overall, the levels of contaminants in water and air are not a [cause] for concern." Once again, PR-speak – a soothing, unquantifiable statement, particularly alarming attached to an ostensible database of unmediated information. "There is no evidence given to support this statement," says Duck. "A scientist wouldn't do this." In fact, he reminds us, the only way to really gather such evidence would require experiments in actual lakes rather than in labs; that is, it would require northern Alberta waters to be studied as closely as those in the Experimental Lakes Area. Plus, monitoring has only recently begun; for 30 or 40 years no such efforts were made, so there's no baseline to serve as a comparison. Years will pass before evidence shows that the environment is or isn't changing, and how, and why.

When the government denies any significant impact, "Well, they're lying," says Donahue. "That's the simple way to say it."

THE BIG PICTURE is that our political leaders – federal and provincial – are wilfully ignoring, distorting and stifling scientific research, especially about human impact on the environment. They're also impeding dissemination of the results of that research and failing to apply those results to policy-making.

"Policy development is insanely complicated," Duck acknowledges, but "trying to cut out science, trying to cut out the way that we discern truth from fiction, is very regressive. It's very backwards thinking. And I don't think this country wants to go back in time." According to Schindler's picture, though, Canada has already time-travelled to the Dark Ages. Schindler says he has never seen any country exhibit "such a shallow understanding of what science entails." In his inimitable disgusted tone, he adds, "Even three or four years ago, I could never believe Canada could sink this low. We're at the bottom of the barrel."

So, are we Canadians, we Albertans, doomed – is evidence-based policy-making really dead? Will we stand by, soothed by ads featuring lush green boreal landscapes, while every last penny, every last drop of oil, is pushed and squeezed and sucked from the land, leaving who knows what mess? Not if we pay more attention, Donahue says, and stop drinking the Kool-Aid. Advocates such as Katie Gibbs and Bill Donahue and outspoken academics such as David Schindler and Tom Duck are working hard to inform us.

We need to demand the resuscitation of public science, to demand facts instead of propaganda – we need to hold our leaders, federal and provincial, to account.

"I'm Trying to Explain Something
That Can't Be Explained":
On Bob Dylan and Big-Ass Truth

LEWIS MACLEOD

> Q: *"How many indie hipsters does it take to screw in
> a lightbulb?"*
> A: *"It's a very obscure number; you've probably never
> heard of it."*

THERE'S A PASSAGE near the end of Bob Dylan's *Chronicles*
in which Dylan and Dave Van Ronk get in a little snit about
the merits of Robert Johnson. The young Dylan is blown
away by Johnson. After hearing Johnson for the first time,
Van Ronk declares Johnson to be "powerful" but derivative. To Dylan's dismay, Van Ronk keeps "pointing out that
this song comes from another song and that one song [is]
an exact replica of some other song." To make his case, Van
Ronk pulls out a variety of older recordings, each designed
to demonstrate some un- or under-acknowledged precursor
of Johnson's. "Dave didn't think Johnson was very original,"
Dylan writes, "I knew what he meant, but I thought just the
opposite. I thought Johnson was original as could be, didn't
think him or his songs could be compared to anything." He
concludes the episode by saying, "there was no point arguing with Dave, not intellectually anyway."

Well, I'm an intellectual, I'm afraid. Arguing intellectually is sort of my job. I make my money as a professor

and literary critic. I get rid of it buying records, instruments and gear, making recordings, booking invisible shows in bars nobody ever goes to, trying in my thirties to do the musical basic-training I never managed to do as a teenager. I love music more than I love literature, but love isn't always returned, as most of us learn at one point or another. Loving something that doesn't love you back has its perks, though; you end up in positions sensible people know enough to avoid, and you, maybe, see things there you don't find elsewhere. It's not an especially ennobling experience for a middle-aged, middle-class Dad to be dumping collected change from a beer pitcher onto a table at 3 a.m. so he can split $150 worth of donations five ways, but I must (I tell myself) be doing it for reason. Right? The only thing that saves the whole project from being a midlife crisis is that it's been so ongoing, so chronic; it started early and doesn't seem especially treatable. This isn't really what Eliot meant when he said we're "only undefeated because we have gone on trying," but I hear that phrase in my head more than I imagine is standard.

I love this exchange between Van Ronk and Dylan for many, many reasons, but I bring it up here because I think it speaks to Dylan's position in the musical culture of the past half century, especially as regards the legitimacy or illegitimacy of intellectual comparison as an aesthetic or evaluative tool. To Van Ronk, Johnson's merits and demerits are a straightforward matter of mapping his contributions against the existing data. If an original contribution can be located, Johnson's stock goes up; if not, not. Comparison is the name of the game. To Dylan, Johnson's achievement comes from the feeling that he sounds as if he "could have sprung from the head of Zeus in full armour," the sense that there are "big-ass truths wrapped in the hard shell of nonsensical abstractions." It doesn't take an especially penetrating analysis to recognize that the armour of nonsensical abstraction is part of Dylan's stock-and-trade, but there's something compelling and unnerving about the idea that "big-ass truth" must necessarily belong to a world that can't be compared to anything else, to forces beyond the situating functions of comparison and analysis. For Dylan, Johnson's apparent lack of originality is a marker of his big-assedness, of both his timeless scope and tectonic rootedness. To Dylan, Van Ronk's vision of originality amounts to something more like "novelty." It's not that Johnson *fails* to make a new contribution to modern music; he bypasses modernity altogether, as a dead-end or maybe a non-starter. To Dylan, at least, the songs aren't "original" in Van Ronk's sense precisely because they're "elemental in meaning and feeling and [give] you so much of the inside picture." This is so much the case, Dylan thinks, that "there's no guarantee that any of his lines either happened, were said, or even imagined."

I call this a movement out of musical history into the world of myth, a world which dissolves the apparent distinction between events that happened and/or didn't happen in light of some wider, more encompassing, vision of "being."

I

ALMOST EVERYBODY I know who ever cared about music got very excited about it very young; we got *really* on top of things as teenagers and this lasted into our early or mid-twenties, when we knew as much about indie or underground bands as keen ten year olds know about baseball stats. Later, everybody who didn't give up altogether started some kind of supplementary, remedial study program: in blues, in jazz, in various visions of folk or "world" (is other music from space?) or whatever. Basically, "the inside picture" gradually became a matter of tracing buried trails rather than identifying rising comets or finding new stars; it became tied to down-and-outers more than up-and-comers. These days, if you want to hold your head up in the 2 a.m. conversations, you're better off referring to something from 1920 than from 2012. This is all pretty standard, I think.

I'll be forty next year; I feel old and I *am* cranky. It's not really surprising that I think there's something undignified about being a scenester beyond a certain age. When I show up at certain bars these days (to play or to listen), I steel myself with some idea that I'm "in it," but not "of it." Almost everybody I know does the same thing. I understand this distinction is weak and self-motivated, but I do think there's a point at which the thoroughgoing now-ness which fuels pop music ought to start to feel a bit weird. It's a good sign if its now-ness falls out of synch with the "then-ness" of getting old, because the self-confident and self-contained temporal bubble of youth must necessarily burst; if you're really lucky, maybe you get a slow leak. More to the point, once you become aware of the bubble, it can only be maintained by denial or drugs. Otherwise, it gets harder and harder to be wholly "in the moment," to deny the current moment's links with what came before and what comes next. Hence, the transition into anthropological or archeological back-study, as a way of figuring *your* musical "now" in terms of some more rooted musical "then."

Dylan's affection for Johnson is linked to his sense that Johnson had "an inside view," and this sense of being "in the know" is obviously part of what fuels most conversations of the type: "have you read?," or "have you heard?" Having access to more than the standard information has a status-enhancing quality that most of us enjoy, but the value of being an "inside" depends a lot on the dimensions and the entry points of the room you're getting into. The hipster joke above (which I love) is aimed at early adopters, scenesters. They're ahead of the curve but not, I'd say, "inside" because the front door and back doors are always open. Their status-enhancing advantage, their version of "inside," is mostly (maybe entirely) temporal; they know sooner, not better, and the room they think they're in doesn't have any solid walls; it's a lean-to, designed to be torn down and rebuilt annually. In 2013, knowledge of the upstart bands of 2008 is worth nothing; everybody's moved on, and nobody's hung back.

Zygmunt Bauman (a wizard of penetrating insight and elegant prose, a Zeus for those interested in intellectual inquiry) makes a wonderful distinction between the logic of beauty and the logic of fashion, one which speaks to both the Van Ronk/Dylan discussion and the hipster issue above. For Bauman, the pursuit of beauty "in its orthodox sense" involved some effort at "eternal duration," at an aesthetic aimed at a "perfection which would put an end to change." This is what Keats meant when he wrote, "a thing of beauty is a joy forever." Both Keats and Bauman are keen on a "loveliness [which will] never pass into nothingness," but the "it" girls (or "it" boys/bands/restaurants/authors) of contemporary culture ought to know that newness and nowness are doing the heavy lifting for them. "No one is expected... to remember today yesterday's talk-of-the-town," Bauman says, and "no one is expected, let alone allowed to steer clear of the talk-of-the-town today." Under such conditions, he thinks, "the link between beauty and eternity, aesthetic value and durability" comes under real pressure. In most cases, it collapses into fashion; the result is that "the beautiful is bound to turn ugly the minute the current fashion is replaced, as it surely will soon be." That's what "cold product" is: last season's beauty. In contrast, when we speak of "a Roman nose" or "Greek proportions," we're not talking about a individuated object so much as enduring type, something seen more than once because its appeal and its duration aren't defined or limited by singularity. This beauty can't get cold because it was never hot; it doesn't participate in that kind of discussion.

I think these temporal terms are worth considering in the current context in which popular music seems stuck between "classic rock" (which trades on evocations of a very specific, bounded past) and multiple visions of the "cutting edge" (which trade upon variously articulated senses of nowness). In either case, the temporal bubble is problematically maintained, either as the discontinuous "then" of the Good Old Days, or as the scenester's discontinuous "now." What Dylan hears in Johnson, and what others now hear in Dylan, I think, is a sound which is neither "now" nor "then," which can never become dated because it sprung from Zeus' head rather than some guy's studio. It appears to originate in some alternate timespace, and, as a consequence, to require an approach outside established interpretive strategies. Van Ronk's assessment of Johnson is explicitly temporal and, to Dylan, consequently misdirected; for Van Ronk, everything that comes first takes precedence over everything that comes next, and can be evaluated as either original or derivative. If some error in dates were to be discovered, and Johnson's recording determined to precede the ones in Van Ronk's collection, Johnson's record would still *sound* the same, even though it would *be* better to Van Ronk. What both Dylan and Bauman point to is, first, a sense of aesthetic value outside any notion of chronological progress or sequence, and, second (and more provocatively), an interpretive position in which a lack of differentiation from one's predecessors (*sameness* not originality) is regarded as an aesthetic achievement.

These issues are at the heart of almost all critical reactions to Dylan's last several records. They're either unoriginal to the point of plagiarism, or so elementally true they can't be compared to anything else.

I'm really interested in the idea of permanent, elemental beauty, but some samenesses *are* just boring and unoriginal, right? How do we differentiate between good and bad sameness, between an eternal, elemental utterance (a big-ass truth) and simple inability to bring anything new to the table? Is it a process or a first-principle kind of thing?

II

LISTEN, I KNOW about sequence and chronology. I had the idea for this essay long before *Tempest* came out and I just never got around to it. Now that I'm doing it, it's been a real drag to read through the recent eruption of essays and reviews, to watch various corners of my argument get claimed by other people, to feel my idea move from moderately original to significantly (though not hopelessly) derivative. It's obvious that nobody's going to interpret the sameness of my position as a sign that I've tapped into some great enduring mystery. But essays like this are never really candidates to traffic in big-ass truth; the stakes are never going to be that high. Everybody knows from the outset what type of interpretive strategy applies to something like this, and it's a Van Ronkian one.

Everybody also, it seems, knows how to read a Dylan record. Mythically.

I haven't done anywhere near all the research, but it doesn't take long to see how Dylan's vision of Johnson saturates current interpretations of Dylan himself. The equation whereby "derivative" is refigured as "mythic and elemental" informs almost everything I've read (and more conversations than it's worth recounting). A few very recent examples: in *Rolling Stone*, "historical accuracy is beyond the point" when evaluating the "prayer of [a] great artist. In *The Atlantic*, "he has always written songs that are designed to transcend the context in which they were created." In *Prefix*: when Dylan sings a cover "he never [sounds] more like himself." There are many more where these came from.

The question I'm asking here is, "How is this done?" How is the suspension of standard evaluation achieved? Given the otherwise thoroughgoing emphasis on nowness and the pervasiveness of "What's Hot / What's Not" visions of beauty, how does the Bauman / Keats / Johnson vision of beauty (a mythical, transcendental, ahistorical vision) become the default interpretive position for Dylan?

I know, I know, he's a legend, but that legend originated in his singular and original contributions as a songwriter. He got to that position because he *wasn't* (or wasn't seen to be) derivative at all. In short, he got here through the discourse of "now."

By way of demonstration, let's return to poor me for a second, toiling as I am under standard, Van Ronkian, comparative analysis. Getting a stable academic job at this point in time (and, really, for the last twenty-five years or so) is a difficult business. There are more candidates and fewer jobs than ever before. I had to work pretty hard to get this university gig, and I'm very happy to have it; I also think I'm good at it. When people don't think I'm any good, there's a great big file in the department office to show them that, actually, I am. In my real job, everything we publish is supposed to be "an original contribution" to knowledge. I'm not sure that's always the case, but that's the organizing idea. If it's not original enough, it's either plagiarized or just "unpublishable." What counts as original to some, of course, sometimes seems self-evident or obtuse (choose your own critique, here) to others. I don't make any absolutist defense, but there are all kinds of credentialed referees to manage the process, from first year composition all the way down the line. As with any scenario of this type, some people think the referees don't know what they're talking about. Fair enough, but the bare fact that it *is* refereed is beyond dispute. The critique/contempt of academic criticism from both arty (lefty?) types and hardcore Harper reactionaries isn't always entirely unjustified, but I think it's often disingenuous and, well, really easy.

It fuels itself on the tedious, incremental nature of academic credentials and on the default situatedness of teachers, the degree to which they're so embedded in the banalities of everyday life. There's no big-ass mysterious truth associated with becoming a professor, just a lot of A-level grades and a few degrees. Because the source and limits of this authority are so prosaic everybody else gets to claim they're drawing their authority from some other, deeper, source. Both "real" artists and "real world" business types tend to see academics as bureaucratic bean-counters, permanently alienated from both real power and knowledge, from the inside picture Dylan finds in Johnson. When people want the inside picture, it's almost never the inside of a classroom or a library.

Now, Robert Johnson, he got to do his job by selling his soul to the devil at the crossroads and Dylan, apparently, derives some of his power from the fact he was "transfigured" when a member of the Hell's Angels, named Robert

Zimmerman, died in a motorcycle accident. You don't get much cooler, or less traceable, than these two as far as credentials go.

I'm no theologian, but I suspect there's really no way to compare one Satanic selling of the soul with another one. Each Satanic pact is its own special snowflake, each transfiguration of a soul a singular event; the guy who tries to put them onto a grid is using the wrong tools. Revelatory access to authority is always less bounded than any situated process; it defies access and in so doing defies evaluation, or, at least, *negative* evaluation. You don't tend to hear people saying, "your Satanic pact is so lame compared to mine."

The literary theorist Thomas Pavel gets very close to the issue when he says that "the mythological mind" distinguishes "between at least three kinds of statements: factual statements, which cover everyday life, true statements, referring to gods and heroes, and fictions, which include stories other than myths (fables, funny moral stories)." In the setup I'm using, then, the "real life" of the artist and/or business type finds his/her primary referent in a rooted factuality (in the way things *really* are), which is then contrasted with the insular artificiality of the academic (who fails to grasp this basic reality and lives in the make-believe world of the ivory tower). This basic distinction between real and bullshit, between fact and fiction, still leaves room for a third, big-ass, category, which is truth. And this truth, to borrow from Hopkins, is, perhaps "past change;" it doesn't traffic in differentiated, "dappled things;" it leaves that kind of stuff aside.

Pavel goes on to say that "societies that believe in myths unfold at two different levels: the profane reality, characterized by ontological paucity and precariousness, contrasts with a mythical level, ontologically self-sufficient, containing a privileged space and a cyclical time. Gods and Heroes inhabit the sacred space [which] is endowed with *more* weight and stability than the mortals' space." I don't think ours is a society that especially believes in myth, but I think it's still one that knows of myth, and, perhaps, *wants* to believe in it in selective rather than all-encompassing ways. It wants to believe in people and spaces that carry more than average weight. Dylan has positioned himself so as to negotiate the divide between a profane reality and an ontologically self-sufficient space. He takes the self-evidently populist (and consequently temporal, profane) mode of popular song and refigures (transfigures?) it as myth, creating a gap between two obviously opposed strategies of interpretation. When a Dylan song sucks as a popular song (or seems plagiarized, etc.) there's a pronounced tendency to re-process it as something "other" than a popular song, as something beyond its interpretive strategies.

In another essay, Bauman, through Nietzsche, focuses on what he calls the "ascetic priests" of the philosophical tradition, those who have managed some kind of "purificatory procedure" which makes them "fit for [...] intercourse with something Wholly Other." Obviously, Johnson's Satanic pact and Dylan's transfiguration involve intercourse with some kind of transcendental "otherness," and this transcendental otherness works to suspend ordinary interpretative procedures. More importantly, the true cleric can't be evaluated in terms of his original contributions because his very "oneness" with other prophets speaks to the enduring (beautiful, true) nature of his project, to his nearness to Zeus' head. In this scenario, each rearticulation both reinforces and enlarges the mythology the ascetic priest embodies and encodes. This is precisely what Dylan means in the recent *Rolling Stone* interview in which he claims first to be "trying to explain something that can't be explained," before going on to refute (profane, prosaic, factual) charges of plagiarism by referring to the "rich and enriching tradition" of which he's a part.

This is all pretty interesting, but I find the idea of *procedures* of purification even more so because it suggests some notion of incremental, rather than revelatory, access to the realm of the wholly other. When the young Dylan first encounters Johnson, he feels both the mythic otherness of Johnson (Johnson makes Dylan feel as if "a ghost had come into the room, a fearsome apparition") as well as his own low-grade factuality, his own rootedness in the everyday life. "I didn't have any of these dreams or thoughts," he writes, "but I was going to acquire them." The "how" of this acquisition is never really covered, of course, but it's safe to say the procedures are more special and esoteric than those involving the rites of, say, transubstantiation. There's no seminary for this kind of stuff, and in the absence of any established acquisition process, Dylan simply emerges (or seems to emerge) with both mythic purchase and a mythic persona somewhere further down the line. So much of Dylan's affect depends upon what we think of this mythic acquisition, where we place, how we interpret it.

And, not surprisingly, many, probably most, of Dylan's detractors zero in on what they regard to be the bogus nature of this claim. Proximity is the enemy of myth. If somebody tells me God appeared to Moses in the form of a burning bush thousands of years ago, I think, "Maybe, I have no idea; things were probably weird back then." If somebody says the Devil appeared before a young guitar player at some Mississippi crossroads in the '20s, I think more or less the same thing at a lower volume. If my roommate tells me he sees Jesus' face in his pizza, I just laugh or check the liquor cabinet.

I don't regard my roommate as a fit candidate for mythic interpretation. He's way too much "here" to be "out there." For this reasons, I see the easy and casual denigration of, say, Mormonism and Scientology as having has less to do with odd religious principles (all religions are a bit weird, right?) than with accessibility and identity. It's not that they're too weird; it's that they're not weird enough. Religions founded by people who have birth certificates seem weird because those guys are too knowable; they're too traceable to historical positions in profane, or maybe more significantly, mundane reality. Joseph Smith and L. Ron Hubbard seem to have more in common with our roommates than they do with Moses. Hell, Hubbard probably had to climb the rope in grade-school gym.

It's no surprise, then, that Dylan's contemporaries regard him with more suspicion than either his early, overzealous, fans or his later acolytes. To most people, Dylan is either too high up or too far back to be approached directly. To Van Ronk, though, "Bobby," is just a pushy kid who stole his version of "House of the Rising Sun." To Joni Mitchell, "everything about Bob is a deception [...] He is not authentic at all." Paul Simon's early Dylan parody, "A Simple Desultory Philippic," mocks Dylan's stock recourse to ostentatious and incoherent non-sequitur as a sign of Dylan's pretentious bullshittedness more than otherworldly or elemental channelling. The "nonsensical abstractions" that Dylan so loves in Johnson, are, to use Dylan's own terms, "pure hokum" to the people who grew up beside and around him, who see him as a pompous roommate, not a special soul.

Paul Simon is a really instructive example here. Both the success and duration of Simon's career as well as his creative output are very similar to Dylan's, yet both his stance and the interpretative stance he tends to provoke are very, very different. Simon's written several really good songs, and some pretty bad ones, but he himself has *always* been a kid born in Newark and raised in Queens. He has talent rather vision, maybe, and it's so, so easy to imagine him with his guitar and his pencil working away, crossing things out then sticking them back in; taking a break, eating a sandwich, falling asleep watching baseball on TV. All the regular evaluative tools always apply to him, and no reviewer quakes before his new release with any emperor's new clothes fear. If Simon's going to be good, we'll always be able to point to what, exactly, we regard as good, and it will always have something to do with the Van Ronkian analysis outlined above. That's because he's from here, not "out there."

III

WHICH BRINGS ME, finally, to the sad case of Jonah Lehrer, onetime wunderkind of *Wired* and *The New Yorker*, currently disgraced, as far as I can track it, for making stuff up in a book about creativity. Lehrer's now-recalled book, *Imagine: How Creativity Works*, purported to explain the neurological and habitual features of the creative process, and to dispel the notion that creativity was a "'gift' possessed by the lucky few." Lehrer's publishers saw the book as a "sparkling and revelatory" effort to shatter "the myth of muses and higher powers." The problem was that Lehrer needed an ascetic priest to stabilize his populist claim. He needed somebody "wholly other" to strengthen his claim that we're all creative. He could only debunk "myth-as-lie" ("It's false that only some people are creative.") through recourse to myth-as-truth ("A Higher and eternal power confirms this to be so."). It's really tough to be "revelatory" without recourse to "higher powers," and the higher power Lehrer went to was Dylan. Lehrer was and is "one of us;" he could see Van Ronk staring over his shoulder, so, when he needed some kind of compelling and semi-coherent statement about the mysterious realm of some kind of creative elsewhere, it's entirely understandable that he'd choose to make up some kind gnomic quote and attribute it to Dylan. He couldn't really say, "It came to *me* in a vision on a mountaintop," but invoking Dylan renders the incoherent coherent, the commonplace profound. Why would Lehrer fabricate something as banal as, "It's a hard thing to describe. It's just this sense that you got something to say," except that he knows it *sounds* different coming from Dylan? Do Dylan's recent recordings sound different based on a similar principle?

What's clear to me is that Lehrer understood both that *he* had to make sense and that Dylan didn't; he was entirely right to think so. He correctly assessed their relative positions in the worlds of fact and myth. What he miscalculated were the bridges which connect these worlds. The problem for Lehrer was that, even though Dylan may be from "out there," his quotations are very much from "here;" they're regarded as missives from the beyond in which Dylan resides, curated, catalogued and puzzled over by his devotees. The triangulation here is as beautiful as it is brutal. Lehrer needed a mythic figure and picked one who readily disappears into a mist, but he failed to account for that figure's traces in profane reality. Importantly, the charge against Lehrer doesn't originate as plagiarism or misattribution; it begins as heresy, noticed by a devoted monk. Michael Moynihan didn't notice the fabrications because he was employed as a publisher's fact-checker (no employee's gonna get this stuff). He wasn't interested in professional misconduct, but divine revelation. He'd internalized the Dylan scripture and, knowing not from whence Lehrer's wisdom came, he did seek the source, saying, "Wherefore came thee to know these mysteries?" Lehrer couldn't answer and Humpty came tumbling down.

(SIDENOTE: One of the less sinister, and, to me, less interesting, lines of argument against Lehrer is that he's "recycled" material from earlier essays in later ones. This, I don't get. I recycle ideas all the time, because I still *believe* them; I still think they work; I still think they're true. I first used the stuff from Pavel in a dissertation I completed ten years ago. I've used it a bunch of times since, whenever I think it's relevant to the discussion. Is the pursuit of novelty so pronounced that it's now regarded as unethical to express the same idea more than once?)

We all get it, Lehrer screwed up. I'm not defending him; he's not even really relevant to this discussion. But just imagine if, when the original scandal was brewing, Dylan had issued a statement of the type: "I've never publicly made the statements attributed to me by Jonah Lehrer. I have never met Jonah Lehrer, but I believe him to be a true spirit, a guy who understands the great currents, the spirit that makes us people, not things. I don't know how Jonah caught hold of them, but I've muttered every word he says I did, and I'd be glad if people take them to be mine. People ought to leave him alone if they think he's misrepresenting me. He's got me as right as anybody. Righter than me." That wouldn't be even a little bit weirder than any number of his previous statements, and my very real feeling is that such a statement would have mitigated Lehrer's position, would have dampened the enthusiastic certitude of Lehrer's detractors, wrong-footed fact-checkers through an appeal beyond facts. I can't think of any other public figure who could chasten self-identified realists through an offhand invocation of powers they *know* they don't know about.

It's all about secular funerals in the end; when I hear Paul Simon songs at funerals I see L. Ron Hubbard standing up at the front with him, eating a sandwich. I see guys from *here* who are just like me trying to explain something neither they nor I can contemplate directly. When I hear Johnny Cash read from the Book of Revelation, I'm prepared to entertain the idea that he might be seeing or hearing something I'm not. I *know* that's because one guy's tall and one guy's short, one guy's dead and one guy's living, one guy's from rural Arkansas and one guy's from Newark, but until such a time as the world comes to be fully under my jurisdiction and understanding, I feel drawn toward remote figures when I try to negotiate remote territories. A lot of good music speaks to the way we live; some of it doesn't.

Richard Rorty has described contemporary secularism in terms of an ever-increasing move toward self-sufficiency. These days, he says, people have an ever-greater "willingness to take [their] chances, as opposed to trying to escape [their] finitude by aligning [themselves] with infinite power." I think he's right, but embracing finitude self-evidently means embracing limitation, and embracing limitation ought to involve an acceptance of signals that evade our limited field of understanding, an acceptance that we're not – and can never be – omniscient. To me, a figure like Dylan speaks to a continued desire to "give over," to trust that some people have access to big-ass truth if not infinite power, and people *like* to align themselves with such figures. Rorty claimed that he himself was "religiously unmusical" the same way other people might be colour blind or unable to smell, that he didn't "get it" even if though he could see other people did.

When I play music, it's almost always with players who are better than I am, and it sometimes happens that, when I think things are sounding OK, somebody will stop and say, "You were late," or "That was flat." The other guys will agree or disagree. When this happens the limits of my own powers of observation are brought home to me in pretty clear ways, and I'm usually compelled to accept that an event I witnessed but didn't really experience has just occurred. I was there, but I didn't get it. Even when I don't get it, though, I can still observe other people observing things I can't myself observe. Sometimes I think it's a conspiracy against me, and sometimes I think, "Wow, these people see, hear and know so much." I'm not saying these guys are ascetic priests, but you get the idea.

If we can witness things we don't experience, then we might also learn to appreciate them, to affirm things we can't articulate. It's always possible that the thing we don't experience isn't even there, but the experience of observing what we don't observe withstands this ontological problem. The *thing* doesn't need to be there for the event to take place; if my bandmates don't really hear what they say they hear, I've still heard them hearing it a whole bunch of times. The experience of witnessing what we don't witness is no less "real" if we later discover that we've conjured the object of that experience. Anybody who's ever been in, or out, of love can tell you that. If Dylan is insincere, his devotees certainly aren't. He can be a fraud without vitiating their experience, and their experience, like Dylan's with Johnson, speaks to a desire for a different kind of "good," a good with more weight and less novelty. The "good" of Van Ronk is the *normal* good, the good of "dappled things;" its beauty is in its uniqueness and its differences, in the feeling of, "Wow, I never saw it quite like that before." This good belongs to time, and as Van Ronk is at pains to point out, it can be dated, graphed and evaluated. Beyond this, there might also be a good that is "past change," that evades time and standard forms of evaluation, that appeals not to what we know and experience but to what we don't know and can't experience.

Because it's all happening on the other side of the curtain, it might be a load of bullshit, as well. But I still don't want to miss it. I don't even really know where Dylan fits in all of this, but I know he makes me think about these issues more than anybody else. I guess that's kind of obvious.

"PIED BEAUTY"
– Gerard Manley Hopkins

Glory be to God for dappled things –
For skies of couple-colour as a brinded cow;
For rose-moles all in stipple upon trout that swim;
Fresh-firecoal chestnut-falls; finches' wings;
Landscape plotted and pieced – fold, fallow, and
        plough;
And áll trádes, their gear and tackle and trim.

All things counter, original, spare, strange;
Whatever is fickle, freckled (who knows how?)
With swift, slow; sweet, sour; adazzle, dim:
He fathers-forth whose beauty is past change:
            Praise him.

When the Vikings Were in Nunavut

MARGO PFEIFF

"LOOK AT THIS!" says Patricia Sutherland. It's 2002 and she's kneeling on the tundra, pointing her trowel at a whale bone at the bottom of the muddy trench she's been excavating. The bone has been fashioned into a spade to cut sod into building blocks, the kind of artifact she would expect to find in old Norse sites in Greenland. To Sutherland, one of Canada's top Arctic archeologists, the sodchopper isn't the only thing that seems out of place at the Nanook archeological dig. Here on the treeless barrens just outside Kimmirut, Nunavut, the structure that she's unearthing – a large, rectangular foundation of rock and sod – just doesn't fit with the landscape.

That's exactly what American archeologist Moreau Maxwell thought when he first began digging here in the 1960s. "He couldn't explain the structures he was finding," says Sutherland. "He said it was complicated."

Complicated – that's exactly what Nanook has proven to be for Sutherland, a former curator of archeology for Ottawa's Museum of Civilization. But now, after seven summers of excavation here, and 12 years of meticulously poring over artifacts and piecing together clues, she thinks she's got the site figured out.

She says that here, on southern Baffin Island, was a trading post occupied by the ancient Norse. Her theory is controversial. But if it's correct, it could rewrite the history books.

IT'S LONG BEEN known that the Norse were active in the far reaches of the North Atlantic. About a millennium ago, seafaring Norwegian traders, some worshipping Odin and others having converted to Christianity, island-hopped in search of resources. They sailed from Scandinavia to the Shetlands, Orkney Islands, Ireland, the Faroes, Iceland, and finally to the western shore of Davis Strait, where colonies were established by Erik the Red, a convicted murderer and charismatic marketer. He named this new place "Greenland," convincing settlers to join him in the protected fjords of the island's southwest. For centuries, the Norse thrived there, supporting themselves by farming and sending trade goods to Europe – everything from walrus ivory to live polar bears for Old World royal courts.

It was during the colonization of Greenland that the snow-capped mountains of Baffin Island were most likely sighted far to the west. A cryptic reference to Baffin was first penned by a 14th-century Icelandic scribe who recorded events that had taken place more than two centuries earlier. In the "Saga of Erik the Red," Erik's adventurous son, Leif Erikson, sailed westward from Greenland around 1000 AD, soon encountering a desolate stretch of land. Rowing ashore, he was unimpressed: "[T]he land was like a single flat slab of rock to the sea. This land seemed of little use." Erikson dubbed it Helluland – "land of stone slabs" – and turned his back on it, heading southwards. Soon he found Markland ("land of forests," possibly Labrador) and then Vinland ("land of wine" or "of pasture" – Newfoundland). At a site now called L'Anse aux Meadows, he built a small station for repairing ships and gathering cargo before returning to Greenland the following spring. Helluland barely received another mention, and by the mid-1400s, the Norse had vanished even from Greenland.

Despite this, or perhaps because of it, whispers of Norse in Canada's Northland have lingered for centuries. Mentions of "blonde Eskimos" appeared from 1821 onwards in the journals of explorers William Parry, John Ross, John Rae and John Franklin. In 1910, Arctic ethnologist Vilhjalmur Stefansson, an Icelandic-Canadian, wrote in his diary about an isolated group of tall Inuit on southwest Victoria Island: "There are three men here whose beards are almost the colour of mine, and who look like typical Scandinavians." But DNA testing on the Victoria Islanders revealed no Nordic genes.

In the 1970s, archeologist Peter Schledermann of the Arctic Institute of North America found Norse artifacts at several sites on Ellesmere's east coast. There were knife blades, pieces of oak with inset wooden dowels, copper, medieval chainmail, ship rivets and woven woollen cloth. These relics dated from between the 13th and 15th centuries, many proven to have originated in Norse settlements in southern Greenland. Fragments of objects made of smelted metal have also turned up on Bathurst and Devon Islands. Had Inuit or their predecessors, the Dorset, scavenged them from Norse shipwrecks? Had they journeyed to Greenland and brought them back? Or had the Norse themselves come here, seeking to trade?

Not long ago, this last theory was commonly accepted: The Norse had ventured west, possibly well into Nunavut, Nunavik and the Gulf of St. Lawrence, to exchange goods with the aboriginals of North America. "But that idea fell out of favour," says Sutherland. So it was controversial when Newfoundland's L'Anse aux Meadows was declared to be a Norse outpost. And when National Museum of Canada archeologist Tom Lee announced in the 1960s that he'd uncovered Norse camps on Quebec's Ungava Bay, "he brought the wrath of the entire archeological community on his head," says Sutherland. After that, most scholars shied away.

Then Pat Sutherland came along. In 1977, as an expert in indigenous archeology, she was hired by Parks Canada to do a survey of potential archeological sites in what would become Quttinirpaaq National Park on Ellesmere Island. She'd just arrived when, amidst the lingering June snow, she spotted something lying on a bald patch of tundra. It was a long, thin piece of metal. Not being familiar with Norse artifacts, she had no idea what it was. But the Parks expert to whom she showed it was shocked. "It was one arm of a bronze balance used by professional Norse traders in the Old World for weighing silver," says Sutherland.

Six years later, on Axel Heiberg Island, Sutherland again stumbled across a strange artifact. Carved on a single piece of antler were two radically dissimilar faces – one with typical round Dorset features, and another, long and thin, with what appeared to be a beard and heavy eyebrows. To her it was an iconic portrayal of two very different cultures. She puzzled over it for a long time, and began to rethink the long-held belief that Norse had not crossed paths with the Dorset.

In 1993 Sutherland was invited to join a dig at a medieval Greenlandic farm called Garden Under Sandet in Greenland. Here, she quickly learned about all things Norse. One of the finds made there was part of a loom with threads of yarn still attached. Six years later, while studying artifacts at the Museum of Civilization, she sifted through a collection excavated in the 1970s and 80s by Father Guy Mary-Rousselière, a French-Canadian anthropologist and missionary based in Pond Inlet. She stopped dead at the sight of two soft pieces of yarn, three metres long, that looked exactly like the wool she'd seen in Greenland. Sure enough, when she took them to a textiles expert, they matched precisely with wool woven at Garden Under Sandet in the late 13th century.

Sutherland knew she was on to something. She hunkered down in the museum's collection, searching through more than 15,000 Arctic objects and comparing them to confirmed Norse artifacts from Greenland, Russia and Europe. Over 100 strands of yarn came to light, hailing from previously excavated sites ranging from northern Baffin Island to northern Labrador. The Inuit and their predecessors, Sutherland knew, didn't use wool – but the Norse did, making garments and even sails from it. The yarn was identified as having been spun with a spindle, requiring great skill to bind the short, smooth fibres of wild animals like Arctic hare. It would have been a laborious task, but the result was yarn that was very soft – and very European.

Armed with this knowledge, Sutherland set off in the year 2000 to re-open the most tantalizing site on Baffin Island: Maxwell Moreau's puzzling Nanook dig in Tanfield Valley, about 20 kilometres from Kimmirut. In Sutherland's eyes, Nanook would have been a perfect spot for the Norse: It had ample sod, a sheltered harbour large enough for wooden ocean-going ships, and plentiful wildlife – especially Arctic fox, the same creatures that prompted the Hudson's Bay Company to choose Kimmirut as their first Baffin post. It was barely 300 kilometres from Greenland – two or three days' sailing. "Why people have trouble accepting that Norse would have been here is crazy," Sutherland says.

After six centuries, Helluland was back in the press and Sutherland's fellow archeologists closely followed her progress. "I knew the project was controversial because everything to do with Norse is controversial," she says. "It had the potential to shift the paradigm about what was happening in the Arctic 1,000 years ago."

Known to be single-minded and unflinchingly committed, Sutherland was prepared for the uphill battle. She had received her share of criticism over the years, as is the norm in a field where radical new concepts are fiercely scrutinized. So to test the strength of her own thesis, she analyzed multiple lines of evidence simultaneously. She excavated new artifacts while at the same time working with experts in fields as diverse as Norse architecture, ancient textiles, insect remains and DNA. Her challenge was to build a multipronged case that the ancient Norse had lived in Nunavut.

It wasn't easy. During long days of fieldwork at Nanook, the site became increasingly complex. Moreau Maxwell's excavations had damaged the walls of the mysterious stone dwelling, but she soon discovered a new wall: layers of sod chunks alternating with large stones, some cut and shaped in a style reminiscent of European stone-masonry. Nanook also yielded a trove of artifacts not usually associated with the Inuit or Dorset, including the whalebone spade, and notched wooden "tally sticks" to record trade transactions. There were remains of European rats that couldn't have survived long in the Canadian Arctic, more strands of Scandinavian-style spun yarn, and European whetstones designed for sharpening metal knives that didn't exist in indigenous Northerners' toolboxes. One particularly intriguing item was a carved wooden figure with a beard and heavy ridge over his eyes: either eyebrows or the edge of a cap common among medieval European merchants.

It wasn't a straightforward dig. Among this jumble were classic hunter-gatherer artifacts like fur-cleaning tools and needles – things Inuit or Dorset might use. And there were issues with the radio-carbon dating: results pointing to the 8th century, hundreds of years before the Norse arrived even in Greenland. Part of the problem, says Sutherland, is that "everything on the site was saturated with seal, walrus and whale oil." Marine-mammal materials are known to skew radio-carbon results, dating them too old. The site seems to point at having been occupied several times, and one radio-carbon date confirms Tanfield Valley was occupied in the 14th century, at the very time Norse settlers lived along nearby Greenland.

Sutherland approached the Geological Survey of Canada to unearth more clues. Using a process not commonly employed in archeology, a technique called energy-dispersive spectroscopy, they painstakingly scanned wear-grooves on more than 20 whetstones from Nanook and similar sites, looking for smelted metal. The results were spectacular: microscopic streaks of bronze, brass and smelted iron, forming positive evidence of European metallurgy. To some scholars – even Sutherland's sceptics – this was the smoking gun. She presented her preliminary results at a meeting of the Council for Northeast Historical Archaeology in St. John's in October of last year. Afterwards, James Tuck, professor emeritus of archeology at Memorial University, declared, "While her evidence was compelling before, I find it convincing now."

SUTHERLAND, WITH MORE than three decades of Arctic archeology under her trowel and by now also a research fellow at the University of Aberdeen and an adjunct professor of archeology at Newfoundland's Memorial University, is convinced Nanook was the site of a Norse outpost dating from the 13th century or so. The structures there strongly resemble confirmed Greenlandic Norse sites, right down to the shallow, stone-lined drainage system to funnel water from the site. Sutherland says the stone-and-sod walls seem to have been hastily constructed in comparison to similar buildings in Greenland, perhaps in a race against a rapidly approaching winter. The close proximity of Dorset artifacts and other remains suggests small bands of hunters likely camped nearby.

Sutherland believes the Norse travelled the Baffin and Labrador coasts for roughly 400 years, from AD 1000 to AD 1400, to ply trade. While it's not clear how many Europeans were at Nanook, nor whether they overwintered or just visited during the warm summers, she speculates that it was just one of many sites throughout the region where Norse traded iron and wood for furs and ivory, luxury items coveted in Europe.

If she's right, Nanook would become only the second confirmed Norse site in North America, after Leif Erikson's L'Anse aux Meadows. But while Erikson only stayed for a winter, and had no apparent dealings with the local aboriginals, Nanook is very different.

"The Northern world," says Sutherland, "was not a remote, marginal place 1,000 years ago, where nothing ever happened. The Norse push west from Norway was a commercial enterprise, for resource exploitation and trade. It was the start of early globalization."

FOR THE 63-YEAR-OLD Sutherland, 2012 looked to be her bonanza year: She presented her metallurgy findings and in

November was featured in a major *National Geographic* article. That same month, she was in a documentary broadcast on the popular CBC show *The Nature of Things*.

But in April of that year, she'd been abruptly dismissed from her 28-year-long tenure at the Museum of Civilization, and her Nanook Project had been put on ice. Her husband, legendary Arctic archeologist Robert McGhee, was stripped of the emeritus status the museum bestowed on him in 2008. Neither Sutherland nor the museum will comment on the dismissals at the present time.

Sutherland's firing, coming on the heels of the federal government's roll call of shutdowns, funding cuts, media-muzzlings and layoffs in the science community, created a furor. One of her many supporters, Memorial University's Tuck, speculated to *Macleans* that Sutherland's reinterpretation of Canadian history might not be in tune with the new mandate of her old institution, which is changing its name to the Canadian Museum of History and focusing narrowly on the country's past 150 years. Other rumours are swirling that with the Harper government's ardent focus on Arctic sovereignty, evidence of Norwegians having set up shop in the Arctic a millennium ago might be too inconvenient to tolerate.

For Sutherland, the hardest blow is having been cut off from her 12 years' worth of research material. For now the remarkable Nanook site lies fallow. "More than anything, I want to finish this project," she says. "At this point in my life I feel it's my legacy." The full saga of the Norse on Baffin has waited 1,000 years to be told, but even now, the ending of the story remains a mystery.

The Defector: *Lessons Learned Undercover*

ANN SHIN

DRAGON WAS THE kind of guy who carried three cell phones in his pocket and spoke four languages, none of them very well. But he spoke with a confidence that made you listen. His nickname referred to the mottled tattoo on his shoulder, and he managed to live up to it. Tough and wily, he was a North Korean broker who guided defectors escaping from North Korea into Asia. He liked to call himself a humanitarian; others might say he was a human smuggler.

I wasn't sure what to think of Dragon, but I had hired him and hitched my wagon to his in order to film undercover with his group of escaping defectors. We had travelled 1,400 km from the North Korean border, and had stopped for a night at a small apartment safehouse in central China, a two-bedroom affair with linoleum floors and curtains drawn in every room. It was a relief to be indoors after having been on buses and trains for days. None of the defectors had proper ID and we had been travelling in constant fear of inspections. If discovered, the defectors would have been arrested and deported back to North Korea.

My DP, Stephen Chung, my Chinese soundman and the group sat down on the living room floor to a dinner spread of take-out Chinese food still in plastic containers. Dragon pulled me over to the side room. "I won't be going with you on the van trip tomorrow," he said. Until this point, Dragon had commandeered every transfer, every bus and train. Why would he be quitting us now?

"I'm not going because we need someone around to clean up, in case something happens."

"In case what happens?" I asked.

"Spot checks, police patrols. I mean we scouted already, there shouldn't be a problem; but I'll stay back just in case… you know."

I eyed him warily. This next part of the journey was the longest leg, and the most dangerous. His sudden decision to stay back rang alarm bells for me. Only eight weeks ago, two South Korean journalists had been apprehended with a group of defectors in a passenger van. If we got caught with these defectors in the same private vehicle, we could be seen as abetting illegal migrants. Stephen and I would be detained and questioned by Chinese officials, which was frightening in itself, but it would be even worse for the others. My Chinese soundman would be jailed, and the footage we had hidden in our suitcases would incriminate Dragon and the defectors. I considered calling the whole thing off but when you've come this far in a film shoot, it's hard to back out.

I HAD ORIGINALLY started researching for my documentary *The Defector: Escape from North Korea* several years ago after reading some accounts by defectors. Their harrowing flight to freedom mirrored in a way my family's experience during the Korean War (1950–53). My socialist aunt and uncle suffered greatly for being North Korean sympathizers and ended up fleeing to the North. There they were seen as traitors and were forced to return to the South. Property was confiscated, they were interrogated and tortured and my uncle died.

The story told by North Korean defectors reminded me of this chapter in my family history and I was deeply affected. I started interviewing defectors in North America and learned about a global network of people helping them both within and without North Korea. While it was nearly impossible to film them inside the DPRK (North Korea), I hoped to film aid workers helping defectors in other parts of Asia. However, the church groups and NGOs I met with considered it too risky for us to film them in Asia. The only people who would consider a film crew were "brokers," whom we could hire as handlers.

We entered a second phase of casting, done over long-distance phone calls. If filming a documentary is a leap of faith, then that faith is built on trust that's established between the filmmaker and her subjects. But how do you establish trust with people you haven't met? I talked with several brokers over the phone as we considered various possible escape routes: Mongolia, or across China into Southeast Asia, or attempting by boat to get into South Korean waters. Each route had different risks and associated costs. After deliberating, I decided, sight unseen, to join a broker who was taking a group of five to six young defectors through China into Southeast Asia. That broker was Dragon.

Dragon said his group of defectors had consented to being filmed but we had to heed his instructions; namely, no cell phones and minimal film gear.

Stephen and I decided on DSLR cameras and packed extra batteries and drives, light panels and a portable chroma key greenscreen to have on hand for the interviews. Still, when we arrived in South Korea, Dragon's eyes popped when he saw our bags. "What are you doing, filming a Hollywood movie?!" We had to pare down our equipment and repack. Finally we were ready to set off to meet with the defectors.

We arrived at a small Chinese farmhouse near the border of North Korea, where bleached grey grass lay flat in the fields. Inside the farmhouse a sack of rice was leaned up against the doorjamb. Brown lacquered clay urns were lined up along the wall.

Five defectors were huddled on some rumpled blankets on the floor. They had been waiting for more than a day for Dragon to arrive. As I looked at their faces, I realized that not only did they not expect a film crew, they clearly didn't want to be filmed. Dragon had lied.

I looked at the five morose North Koreans, not knowing what to do. Luckily, the farmhouse owner had cooked up a large pot of chicken congee and he passed around the steaming bowls. We sat down on the floor to eat.

Eating together is perhaps the best way to break the ice on a shoot. Dragon told stories of when he escaped from North Korea and called himself their 'older brother,' saying he'd look after them. He pointed to me, saying I was their 'older sister' from Canada and that I would help them out more than they would know. He charmed everyone, bringing them on side for the sake of the shoot; I was grateful.

One young woman, Sook-ja, shared her moving story about how she escaped across the border to search for her missing sister. Her sister had ended up falling into the hands of Chinese traffickers and Sook-ja was close to despair since none of her contacts in China knew where her sister was now.

Another woman, Yong-hee, had been duped and sold to traffickers by a family friend. Like 80 to 90 percent of North

Korean women defectors, Yong-hee was sold as a bride to a Chinese man. (The gender imbalance in China, caused by their one-child policy, has created a demand for North Korean women.) She ended up in a rural Chinese village where she met other North Koreans, and through word of mouth, she learned about brokers like Dragon.

Trust grows swiftly within a group when there are lives at stake. Over the next few days, we travelled and ate together and the defectors shared their stories. They consented to filming but wanted us to conceal their identities; I assured them we would. Stephen set to work on devising creative ways to film. The DSLR cameras were great as they also enabled us to film in uncleared locations such as trains and bus stations, where we rolled with the cameras slung around our necks. Our soundman cleverly slung his portable recorder in a pouch and simply stood close to people as they spoke.

I became quite attached to Sook-ja and Yong-hee and they with me, so when Dragon decided not to continue on the journey midway, we grew closer. Unlike Dragon, we were new to this journey, and we faced the unknown together. Travelling for days in a group, we separated at the Laotian border, and with the help of Dragon's contacts we arranged to meet in Thailand. The group encountered a few mishaps and were delayed; my opinion of Dragon dropped to an all-time low. When we finally met and embraced in Thailand, I made arrangements with Sook-ja and Yong-hee to meet in South Korea, where they expected to be sent.

MONTHS PASSED AND I heard no news from Sook-ja or Yong-hee. I finally called Dragon in Seoul.

"They're here," he said. "They're in Hanawon, and should be out in a few weeks." Hanawon was the North Korean refugee reception centre in South Korea. Refugee claimants are able to make phone calls, so I wondered why the women hadn't called me.

"Don't worry," said Dragon, "I'll call you when they're released."

True to his word, Dragon called when he found out the day that Sook-ja and Yong-hee would be released. I flew to South Korea and met Dragon, who told me the women didn't want to speak with me. At first I didn't trust him, but he then called them and passed his cell phone over.

"Oh, sister, it's good of you to come all this way," Sook-ja said. "But I can't be in your movie anymore. I heard our families will be severely punished if they know we defected to South Korea."

I was saddened, and conflicted about her change of heart. I cared about her and didn't want to put her family at risk; yet, we had taken precautions to guard her anonymity all along. Nothing had changed in our approach but she had changed her mind.

Then Sook-ja made a request that surprised me. "Dragon's been hounding us for money, sister. Could you speak to Dragon on our behalf?"

"What money?" I asked.

"Broker fees."

It turns out all North Korean defectors accepted into South Korean society are given a government stipend upon release from Hanawon. Most of these funds end up being paid to the brokers they hired. Dragon wanted them to hand over his broker fees.

I hung up and stared at Dragon. Documentary filmmakers aren't supposed to get involved in their stories, I knew this, but couldn't help but ask, "Can't you give these girls a break?"

Dragon blew smoke in the air. "Are you kidding? Most brokers charge $3,000, $5,000. I'm asking way less. They knew they had to pay a fee but now that they're here, and free, they don't want to pay."

I sat with this. Dragon, in his own way, was principled. True, he ferried defectors across borders illegally, and where this line of work sits in the moral universe is another complex discussion. But Dragon, like all brokers, took on significant personal risk to guide the defectors. Of course a broker isn't as sympathetic a figure as Sook-ja and Yong-hee. But even Dragon needed to keep his identity concealed, for unlike the other defectors, he would go *back* into China again and again. Despite this, he remained committed to the documentary, delivering everything he said he would. He led the defectors out of China as he promised; now he wanted them to keep their end of the bargain.

Dragon was and still is a complicated figure in a documentary where we were privy to seeing many things considered illegal – including North Korean defectors hiding in China and Laos. As a filmmaker, I tried to portray the complexity of the situation. As a fellow human, I witnessed the courage of a handful of desperate people and found myself swayed by conflicting interests. More than once, this film made me challenge my assumptions and correct my position. It was a dialectic and revelatory process in which I seesawed my way to a new understanding of their world. And isn't that what lies at the heart of documentary filmmaking?

Approaching Infinity

KILBY SMITH-MCGREGOR

Then again perhaps the footnote was in some book that had nothing to do with the Greeks at all.

Many books frequently containing things that are connected to other things that one would have never expected them to be connected to.

Even in these very pages I am writing myself, for instance…

– David Markson, *Wittgenstein's Mistress*

I DROPPED BOTH math and science in high school as soon as was legally allowed – grade nine and ten, respectively. At first I'd been quite taken with the world-shaping premises and clean formalism of these subjects, their elegant equations yielding true and false; right, wrong. Math and science seemed to preside over a pristine realm of quantifiability. Even as an adolescent there was something appealingly aesthetic about that to me. As the operations became more difficult, however, unsettling sorts of indeterminacy and paradox were exposed. I recoiled from the disjunct between the formal limits of mathematical representation and the increasingly complex content which that symbolic language was supposed to represent accurately. In my own unformed way I'd begun to intuit a threat in the chasm between the language of proofs and their apparent matter.

"The mathematics they are studying has become more modern and more abstract, and he has begun to flounder," J.M. Coetzee relates in his 2002 autobiographical novel *Youth*, "Line by line he can still follow the exposition on the blackboard, but more often than not the larger argument eludes him. He has fits of panic in class which he does his best to hide." For my own teenage part, I felt cut loose in these classes and not nearly smart enough to understand whatever it was I was supposed to get or know or, worse, simply accept. So I dropped the subjects. I couldn't handle the dissonance. Or perhaps, at fourteen, I just couldn't work through feeling stupid. There's a bloody-minded extremity in Coetzee that I've always been grateful for, and would never describe as cold, though he and others have; I recognize its likeness, even just barely stirring, in my fourteen-year-old-self: "Never in his life has he had to call on his utmost powers. Less than his best has always been good enough. Now he is in a fight for his life." Barely stirring, but awakened, as I signed my add/drop forms.

I dropped other stuff, fitfully, seemingly anomalously, over the next decade and a half. Out of university, for example, more than once. Opportunities, dreams, responsibilities, people. I let a lot of things go. Somehow I maintained a patina of capability, even achievement; my compensatory patter was convincing enough to draw attention elsewhere, including my own. Dropping things, dropping out, is in no way remarkable. Letting go is part of experimenting, learning, growing up – at least, until it isn't. But the question of what I could or could not handle continued to dog me, and late in the winter of my thirtieth year, it claimed my undivided attention. I experienced a crisis that provided cause enough to start tracing each pinprick flare, those dying stars still charged in memory, of things-let-go. It had escalated gradually. The small and progressively less-so incidences of my dropping things, and the accompanying gestures of withdrawal, had bit by bit given way to a guts-scooped-out dissociative ache, as if everything were already absent – always already absent – inside of me. This sense spawned a loop of doomed reasoning that could only envision an end to, and relief from, its own poisoned involution in blacking itself out. I'd stopped being able to sleep, which had been the first line of defence. Haphazard attempts at hard drinking proved sloppy and unsustainable. And I couldn't interrupt the flood of more dramatic plan b blackout options loudly recommending themselves ad infinitum. On Toronto's Centre for Addiction and Mental Health Emergency room intake form, their definition of emergency is the classically phrased: *danger to oneself and/or others*. You're required to place a checkmark in the box beside this statement while the pre-interview support worker watches you wrestle dumbly with the hospital pencil, trying to make your fingers work like fingers that responded to your wishes or were even part of your body (or at all belonged to you) would. Here they examine your grip, I like to imagine myself thinking in that moment. Of course, there was no thinking, only raw incapacity.

I knew my problem. My problem was everything.

A few years prior to my CAMH visit, nearly twice the age I'd been when I'd broken it off with math, officially, I had sought out the book-length essay *Everything and More: A Compact History of* ∞, part of Norton's Great Discoveries series, by a fiction writer I'd become interested in, David Foster Wallace. With his 1997 one-thousand-plus-page breakout novel *Infinite Jest*, Wallace had well-proven himself both a serious student, and innovator, of infinite regress (and some of its heavier implications for both brains and bodies) in the literary realm. This was the guy a former professor remembers having straightforwardly regarded during his undergrad years as "a philosopher with a fiction hobby." I had emerged from adolescence as an unlikely lay-student of the infinity principle myself; at least I was increasingly drawn to discussions of limits, or lack thereof, how the formation and transgression of boundaries played out in the human world, and the consequences for consciousness, bonds between beings, emotional life, ethics. I'd developed the intuition that my own desire to write literature was tied to a fascination with the limits of natural language, its gap in representing experience – all the uneasy formal indeterminacies, in fact, that had once scared me off mathematics' significantly *less* messy symbolic system. This perverse desire to embrace language as a necessarily tragic imprecision, an awkward expression of thwarted longing and untethered impulse, unmeetable need, bore some resemblance to a compulsion to press my finger deep into a wound.

By this point in my late twenties, owing to the literary acuity of a few generous souls, I'd belatedly been introduced to a string of books that confirmed a charged interest and awareness in me, no matter how arguably perverse. The sudden appearance of Wallace, Coetzee, W. G. Sebald, David Markson, among others, reconstellated literature. The fraudulence paranoia I bore as a would-be writer who secretly hated to read (since I'd never been particularly good at or much interested in that mechanism referred to as plot, upon which the fiction to which I'd previously been exposed all seemed to hinge) evaporated. The paint-by-numbers version of what I'd once resigned myself to accepting as literature had blown its cover, and the bared material beneath shot light in a thousand directions at once. These stories were metaphysically complex in ways I'd never encountered outside the philosophy department (through which I'd bounced briefly after high school), but they were also socially and culturally responsive, *inhabited* in ways that made a haunted house of academic philosophy. Long-suppressed murmurings about perception, mortality, and meaning within me – reframed – became audible, responsive as they were, to being called forth by these unapologetically intellectual, consciousness-driven, and heartbreakingly human narratives I'd begun to take in. To take in, but not wholly process. And if you can imagine, on the one hand, the breathtaking illumination of this immersive reading odyssey, perhaps you can also imagine the shadowlands at its edges, how I could end up identifying with the peripatetic narrator of Sebald's *The Rings of Saturn*, who, recalling his long, solitary rambles through the time-scarred English countryside, states in the opening passage of the novel:

> I have seldom felt so carefree as I did then, walking for hours in the day through the thinly populated countryside, which stretches inland from the coast...
>
> At all events, in retrospect I became preoccupied not only with the unaccustomed sense of freedom but also with the paralysing horror that had come over me at various times when confronted with the traces of destruction, reaching far back into the past, that were evident in that remote place. Perhaps it was because of this that, a year to the day after I began my tour, I was taken into hospital in Norwich in a state of almost

total immobility. It was then that I began in my
thoughts to write these pages.

What Sebald is gesturing to, in a socio-historical context;
what Wallace is after, in his consideration of infinity, is the
slippery nature of not simply cultural memory (in Sebald's
case) or recursive logic (in Wallace's), but more broadly,
abstract thought. Abstraction yields metaphor and further,
identification, the impact of which can stop a body dead in
its tracks. The effect on human consciousness when abstract
reasoning leaps the intellectual realm and insinuates itself
into embodied experience is a particular and peculiar one:
Sebald's "state of almost total immobility." For Wallace:
"Another sure sign it's abstract thinking: you haven't moved
yet." When the borders between thought, feeling, and function all but obliterate themselves, you've got the phenom-
enon of a mental process with a physiological cost. "She
has a headache. Too many heady abstractions," Coetzee's
Elizabeth Costello catches herself thinking: "a warning from
nature." While Wallace observes: "It might be that philoso-
phers and mathematicians, who spend a lot of time thinking
(a) abstractly or (b) about abstractions or (c) both, are *eo
ipso* prone to mental illness. Or it might just be that people
who are susceptible to mental illness are more prone to
think about these sorts of things."

A grad school prof of mine once told us the worst sin
you could commit as a fiction writer was to have a character
alone, thinking. Fair warning. It's a good stock rule for mental
health reasons alone, but I wasn't deterred, even when he'd
write "boring" – and not necessarily without cause – along
certain margins of my class assignments. It's worth the risk
of being boring, of even detours into an interior unhinged.
For some of us, *alone-thinking* is where large parts of our real

true lives happen, and we're driven to attempt to capture the flavour of those real true lives, like all writers, to regift and reconfigure the lost and found items from our own narrow biographies in urgently imagined prose-worlds. It's certainly true that a lot of the time the alone-thinking expression fails in fiction, but occasionally you get a gem that commands the power to make "heads throb heartlike," as Wallace has described the effect of David Markson's 1988 novel *Wittgenstein's Mistress*. If dense, recursive thought is a notable feature of Wallace's own prose, it is perhaps the definitive feature of Markson's very appropriately titled novel, which I tracked down after listening to a discussion between Wallace and Michael Silverblatt on KCRW's *Bookworm*. Here is the edge I'm willing to give English, or any other natural language, over math as a system of representation. It has a face, and by that I mean a voice, the intertwined capacity of intellectual and emotional consciousness, by which I mean – life; a forum to enact what Wallace identifies, in this case, as a "continual struggle against the slipping sand of English & the drowning-pool of self-consciousness." So here is Kate, our Mistress, in an abandoned house, on an abandoned beach – alone, thinking – at the keyboard at the end of the world:

> Actually, I am not feeling tired. How I am feeling is not quite myself.
>
> Well, perhaps what I am more truthfully feeling is a kind of depression. The whole thing is fairly abstract, at this point.
>
> In any case, doubtless I was already feeling this way when I stopped typing. Doubtless my decision to stop typing had much to do with my feeling this way.

I have already forgotten what I had been typing when I began to feel this way.

Obviously, I could look back. Surely that part cannot be very many lines behind the line I am typing at this moment.

On second thought I will not look back. If there was something I was typing that had contributed to my feeling this way, doubtless it would contribute to it all over again.

I do not feel this way often, as a matter of fact.

Generally I feel quite well, considering.

Still, this other can happen.

It will pass. In the meantime there is little that one can do about it.

Anxiety being the fundamental mood of existence, as somebody once said, or unquestionably should have said.

Though to tell the truth I would have believed I had shed most of such feelings, as long ago as when I shed most of my other sort of baggage.

When winter is here, it will be here.

Even if one would appear never to be shed of the baggage in one's head, on the other hand ...

A good deal of one's baggage would appear to be not even one's own, as I have perhaps elsewhere suggested.

What Markson gives us, occupying and dramatizing the form of Wittgenstein's abstract mathematical metaphysics – and Wallace has a lovely way of describing it – is "the difference, say, between espousing 'solipsism' as a metaphysical 'position' & waking up one fine morning after a personal loss and finding your grief apocalyptic, literally millennial, leaving you the last and only living thing on earth, with only your head, now, for not only company but environment & world, an inclined beach sliding toward a dreadful sea." I would further draw attention to the movement of Kate's *Tractatus*-patterned cognition. Her repetition, re-evaluation, self-correction, and specifically the feat of *writing out* these processes, no matter how involuted, is actually a gesture (or at least an inclination) beyond a hermetic self, toward communication, an unflinching, if canted, desire to be accurate, truthful – and finally, *known* – by what real or imagined Other, we need not over-define.

High above another desolate beach, Sebald's narrator, following the edge of Suffolk's coastal cliffs, comes upon a herd of swine lying in a stubbled field. He climbs over the low wire of the electric fence and approaches one, who, at his touch, trembles, sighing "like one enduring endless suffering." Sitting afterward in the grass between fence and cliff-edge, he is taken back to the story of the mad Gadarene in the Gospel of Mark, remembered vividly from childhood, yet having never been satisfactorily explained in his religious education:

> The raging maniac, of whom it is said that he came out of the tombs where he dwelt, was possessed of so violent an unclean spirit that he could not be bound or tamed. He plucked asunder the chains, and broke the fetters in pieces. Always he was in the mountains, writes St. Mark, and in the tombs, crying, and cutting himself with stones. Asked his name he answered: My name is Legion, for we are many.

So what is the nature of this particular, uncontainable, madness? *The that-which-cannot-be-handled* is my favourite DFW colloquialism for the Greek term *to apeiron*, meaning, "not only infinitely long/large but also undefinable, hopelessly complex." He traces its origins to Greek tragedy, "where it referred to garments or binds 'in which one is entangled past escape.'" Infinite bondage: neither a nice thought, nor a new one. The mad Gadarene of the gospel pleads with God to be spared from exile, and in turn, God commands the possessing spirits to enter a herd of swine feeding nearby. "And the swine, some two thousand according to the evangelist, plunged down a steep slope and drowned in the sea," Sebald tells us. If the story's true, he reflects, God comes off as somewhat creepy. Alternately, it's a made-up story serving to "explain the supposed uncleanliness of swine; which would imply that human reasoning, diseased as it is, needs to seize on some other kind that it can take to be inferior and thus deserving of annihilation." Our troubled Sebaldian stares out over the cold German Ocean. Ah. Yes. In the Greek-tragic version, I believe there's a goat somewhere here.

Is it really demon possession, I wonder, to have the experience of feeling "many," or of feeling the grief and unrest of History's limitless wrongs awake in your bones, and brain, somehow, branching out beyond personal biography – that overwhelming feeling which perhaps leads to the crying and the cutting oneself with stones; to the tombs, drawn again and again; to the solitary mountains? Yet it is our oh-so dangerous ability to abstract in such a way that grants us the capacity for empathy, and following from that: conscious community, love, connection. This gift of identification opens in us, when we stand with Sebald, the imaginative possibility of a pig from whose sigh we extrapolate the endurance of endless suffering, who might, as we withdraw our hand, "[close] its eye once more with an expression of profound submissiveness." Sentimental anthropomorphism, I think this isn't, but rather, the same capacity that could lead David Foster Wallace to Consider the Lobster, or Markson's Kate to be moved that: "when Friedrich Nietzsche was mad, he once started to cry because somebody was hitting a horse;" that could lead Coetzee, like Kafka before him, to abstain from eating meat, to draft "The Lives of Animals," then obsessively revisit those lives in *Elizabeth Costello*. The double-edged ability to recognize the existence of consciousness and suffering non-identical to our own – and beyond human terms, in its farthest reaches – launches a chain of correspondence that threatens the implicit practical divisions by which we function and focus in our daily lives. So where must one draw the line, empathetically, between self and other?

The evening following my five hours of interviews and observation at CAMH Emergency – still a shaky, somewhat aphasic, adrenalin-spent creature – I surprised myself by accepting a dinner invitation. I walked south and west through neighbourhoods still spotted with gritty post-snowdrifts to join two longtime friends and their young children for a meal. It was not yet spring. Moving awake through the city on this new next day, though, and for a few days following, some halo effect of those drawn-out hours of on-the-record confession embraced my knotted-up self. Breathing the raw air I experienced a reprieve, release even. I felt beautiful, physically whole, in a way that I haven't before or since. After dinner I lay on my back on the green-and-white floral couch with Kate and Lea's four-year-old daughter, Livia, heavy against my chest and an oversized cardboard-bound book in my hands. Reading aloud, I became slowly aware that this book, with its 1976 Caldecott Medal insignia, had been read to me, also, as a child. Yet I could not remember the events of each chapter until the sentences themselves formed on my lips. Somewhere in the middle of the story, Livia stopped me with an insistent seriousness and we sat up. She held her arm toward me, open-palmed, in a sort of presentational manner by which she supported her own elbow with the other hand. The seriousness was here, in the arm extended soundlessly, and I had the distinct impression of being at a disadvantage in that moment, circumscribed by the expectations of adult consciousness. I would have to be condescended to. Here, she pointed, I'm hurt. Have hurt? A hurt? Am hurt? I can't remember. But she pointed – hurt. And sure enough, in the well between two fingers: once-broken skin now set as a thin, slicing scab. There it was, the site of all seriousness. She tugged my own fingers to touch it. Touch it, she said. She said this word. Touch. *Hurt; touch.* The rest of the award-winning book is a blank.

Later I am alone on the couch, waiting for bedtime to be over; no child, no book. The night is full-on now, and I leave the light off. A thin blanket covers either my feet, or my arms, I must choose. Upstairs, with their two mothers, the two children. I listen to small-person screaming set out against reasoned, compassionate voices. Then a lull. I hear her mother: I know, Livia, I know. Your brother is hurt and now you need to be hurt too. I recalled, then, an open sore on baby Thom's tiny ear, the origin of which my two friends had been puzzling over earlier that evening. What she meant, I assumed, was that she recognized Livia's desire for attention, to be the centre of it, and that this was a defensible childishness, to be reasoned through and grown out of, one would hope. Then something else came to me, lying there in the unlit living room, sprung from what had come before. Livia's demand to be met. *Touch.* My fingers tentatively acknowledging her cut. *Your brother is hurt and now you need to be hurt too.* The impulse, childish or no, is perhaps not only that of self-absorption, but more deeply of other-absorption, a desire to join, know, feel, the inside of another's experience – we may confuse empathy for solipsism. The corresponding desire, is to be known, felt, entirely, indivisible from the world, from all life. The expression *undivided attention* takes on a sacred cast when I place it in this context for myself, caring to name an alternate infinity. I picture Livia, resistant-hot and wet with tears: let me, if only in my mind, if only for this moment, give you my undivided attention. Just for tonight, we'll call it love. "Across what distances in time do the elective affinities and correspondences connect? How is it that one perceives oneself in another human being, or, if not oneself, then one's precursor?" writes Sebald. Across what distances in flesh, body; what divisions of mind, then? And if not one's precursors, one's descendants.

I ride home that night in a cab, heavy-lidded, rattling backward in my thoughts through this long, blinding winter. And I'm given to recall another bedtime story, near the very end of Derek Jarman's 1993 Brechtian hallucination of a film, *Wittgenstein*. From a hooded figure seated in near-darkness by the bedside of the dying philosopher, we hear:

> There was once a young man who dreamed of reducing the world to pure logic. Because he was a very clever young man, he actually managed to do it. And when he'd finished his work, he stood back and admired it. It was beautiful. A world purged of imperfection and indeterminacy. Countless acres of gleaming ice stretching to the horizon. So the clever young man looked around the world he had created, and decided to explore it. He took

> one step forward and fell flat on his back. You
> see, he had forgotten about friction. The ice was
> smooth and level and stainless, but you couldn't
> walk there. So the clever young man sat down and
> wept bitter tears.

Houses, trees, sidewalks zip by in the dark. Streetlights angle
sharply off the breath-fogged pane of my backseat window.
Oblique, I mouth the word; obtuse. I am both and more. I
return again to the once-floundering math student, John of
Youth, who finds himself, at twenty-four, a British Ministry
of Defense computer programmer: "Tests no longer seem to
come with fair warning these days, as they did when he was
a schoolboy, or even announce themselves as tests." Having
fled the cruel binarism of apartheid-era South Africa, now
sick over his implication in the us-them of the British cold-
war effort, he is desperate to find a crack through which he
might escape this divisive mode of being:

> He is reading the history of logic, pursuing an
> intuition that logic is a human invention, not part
> of the fabric of being…
>
> …Most of what he reads he does not under-
> stand, but he is used to not understanding. All he
> is searching for at present is the moment in history
> when *either-or* is chosen and *and/or* discarded.

He will find the opening, driven by intuition past pure
math in pursuit of a different, less determinate, language
template – that of literature. He will write many novels,
many essays. He will win the Nobel Prize in this indetermin-
ate field of human words, of stories. I will learn to sleep and
wake again, to make my way through months darker than

these now past, prescriptions that hurt, then help, chemical compounds and talking cures; a new next season, and another. Tonight, driving home, I trace the tails of lights across the window with my finger; I dream together with Kate, held, at the limit of possibility:

> Winters, when the snow covers everything, leaving only that strange calligraphy of the spines of the trees, it is a little like closing one's eyes.
>
> Certainly reality is altered.
>
> One morning you awaken and all color has ceased to exist.
>
> Everything that one is able to see, then, is like that nine-foot canvas of mine, with its opaque four coats of white plaster and glue.
>
> I have said that.
>
> Still, it is almost as if one might paint the entire world, and in any manner one wished.

What Happens at the End

EUGENE STICKLAND

THIS JOURNEY BEGAN a few years ago with a chance encounter at a Christmas party. Among the people sitting at my table was a doctor from the palliative care unit at the Foothills Hospital. I commented that he must have an interesting job. He knew that I'm a playwright and said the same thing about me. By the end of the evening we had arranged for me to visit the unit to have a look around for myself. Seems like a strange outcome for a Christmas party, but you never know what's waiting around the corner.

Looking back, what surprises me is my willingness to jump in and learn more about something most of us don't really like to think about. I don't like hospitals all that much, or doctors, or the questions they ask, or the tests they want to do on me. Like many men of my age, I prefer not to think about it ... in this case, "it" being a loaded term referring to health, loss of health, onset of disease (probably a grisly one) and, finally, death. Ironically, at the same time, because I have reached a certain age, I can easily convince myself that every little pain I feel, every sore throat I wake up with, is the beginning of the end.

Death actually presented itself to me at an early age – 11 to be precise – when my older brother died in a car accident.

The loss was immense and has no doubt informed much of my character as I have grown older. Obviously, the longer we live, the more family and friends we lose along the way. And yet I suppose that because I was exposed to death at such an early age, it doesn't scare me and I have become quite dispassionate about the matter.

Over the years, I have written about death extensively in my dramatic work; at least five of my plays deal directly with the topic, and one of them is even titled *A Guide to Mourning*. Artists are always looking for new fields to explore, and the field of death – because of its universality and mystery held together in one event – is a particularly rich field to stick our shovels into.

AND SO, ON a cold morning a few weeks into the new year I got myself over to the Foothills and made my way up to the fourth floor of the Tom Baker Cancer Centre. My friend met me and I was soon in a room with members of the palliative care team, which was much larger and more comprehensive than I would have imagined, including, among others, physicians, residents, nurses, pharmacists, therapists, social workers and spiritual counsellors.

What I hadn't realized was just how welcome I would be – not just as a new friend of one of the lead doctors on the unit, but as a writer with a reputation for exploring difficult issues, often ones people simply don't want to talk about. In this case, the big one, I suppose. Not just death in general, but specifically: What does the process of dying look like in our culture these days? What might we be in for as we near the end of our journey? At this point, I might as well step out of my narrative to remind readers that we do, in fact, die. It's the only thing we know for sure about our journey – that it's going to end.

I think as a culture we do an admirable job of staying in denial of this eventuality. I was talking to a man the other day who was speculating on his own demise, which he put some 50 years in the future. He was in his 50s. I suppose as long as we can put an event at least five decades from now, we clearly don't have to deal with it. As it was, I didn't have the heart to tell him that he was, by any meaningful calculation, well beyond middle age. Who am I to burst his bubble?

A variation of this, which I indulge in almost daily, is to read the obituaries in the paper, checking out the birthdates of the dearly departed, comparing them to my own. Most days I successfully perpetuate my delusion of immortality, confirming that only people older than myself are dying and that I am certainly too young to die. But of course the older we get, the more likely we will read about people our age or even younger (or even very much younger) passing away. In the face of such evidence, we might do well to consider and come to grips with the implications.

To put this all in perspective: The average age of the patients in this particular palliative care unit is 51 years old. I find that rather sobering, if not chilling. We reach a certain point when the experience and expected outcome of hospital visits change. When you're younger, you expect to get better and get out. When you find yourself in the hospital and are told you're not going to get better, and face the reality of your imminent demise, then a hospital visit is a much different thing. And it's easier and comforting to think this only happens to older people; not so easy or comforting to get your head around the number 51.

IF WE ARE collectively in denial of the reality of death in the abstract, it can only be worse when it comes to considering the specifics. And so, for a writer to walk into a room full of professionals who work in this area day in, day out, was thought to be a wonderful thing, a great step forward in public relations, as it were. You have to understand that when these people tell others what they do for a living, it can be a bit of a conversation ender.

My reputation was a double-edged sword, however. As much as the staff welcomed my help to bring their work out into the open, when it came to visiting patients – well, not everyone wants a writer hanging around witnessing what is, after all, a very private event.

As I sat among the staff that first morning, on the one hand I knew nothing about palliative care and on the other hand I realized I'm a bit of an expert. Listening to them talking about their work I was flooded with a remembrance of an event that had happened some 17 years earlier: the death of my father in the palliative care ward at the Pasqua Hospital in Regina. I shared that experience with them, for I think at its heart it has to do with the essence of palliation, which means dying in as good a way as possible. It is a story of someone who lived a good life and then, at the end, did a very good job of dying.

We had our usual Sunday evening phone call. I was in Calgary, and my dad and mom were back in Regina. On this particular evening, my dad complained about a sore arm, telling me he had arranged to go for a massage the next day. A few days later, my brother called to tell me the masseuse had not liked something about my dad's sore arm and had suggested he see a doctor. He had done so, and was subsequently admitted to the hospital for tests. On Thursday my brother called to say things weren't looking all that good as the result of these tests. On Friday he called and his message was unequivocal: Get here, now.

I got there, driving through a prairie snowstorm to do so. My dad held on until I arrived, and then, son of an Englishman that he was, shook my hand and promptly slipped into a coma. A few days later, I sat in his room with him in the palliative care ward. I had no idea if he had any awareness of what was going on around him, so I read him the hockey stories from the night before. I was holding his hand, the first and last time that ever happened. As I was doing so, he let out one last rattling breath and then he was gone. In death as in so many aspects of life, my dad was efficient and orderly.

The people from the ward came in just at that moment. When they found out I was alright, they did a few things with my dad, removing equipment, arranging him, as it were, the way I thought we should leave him until my mother had a chance to spend some final moments with him. I suggested staff meet her in the hallway before she got to the room, to let her know what had happened. All of this took place with great reassurance and professionalism, and I would have to say that as far as possible, the staff made a potentially terrible situation really as good as it could possibly have been.

So, looking around that room in Calgary all those years later, I had a good sense of what palliative care workers do, what they are all about. They make dying as good an experience as they possibly can, for all involved. I know that isn't a very technical explanation, but I don't think anyone on the unit would dispute its veracity.

YOU MIGHT DIE on a lonely stretch of highway some night when you hit black ice. You might have a very sudden and very fatal heart attack while riding your bike along the river. Or you might be lucky enough to have the dream death ahead of you, the one I hope is in store for me: you may have a beautiful day doing all of your favourite things and go to bed with a big smile on your face and simply not wake up. It happens, I guess, but only to a few.

But should you be diagnosed with a disease (most likely cancer), which is all the more common these days, and should that disease prove fatal, with no hope of a cure whatsoever, then you will be left in a situation where the rest of your life will be spent dealing with the process of dying. If you have complications, you might find yourself in palliative care with a team to help with any or all of these.

What might those complications be? Pain, too much of it to deal with, and so you might be there on account of pain management. You may have psychological difficulty – after all, death is an enormous thing to get your head around. Even in these times of vague spirituality, we still contemplate what lies beyond death, not just the patient but the family as well. Legal or financial or family issues can complicate matters. In any of these cases, a staff person on the unit can help look after things.

As we all know, given Alberta's ongoing crisis with healthcare funding, long hospital stays are not encouraged, and the best outcome as far as the people who work on the unit are concerned is that once your complications have been dealt with, you go to a hospice or return home, and with the support of community professionals and family get on with the matter at hand, which is to say dying. To put this into perspective, the unit has 29 beds. In 2009 about 250 patients were admitted and the average stay was 12 days. One in every four patients died on the unit.

On the day of my first visit, one of the doctors invited me to spend some time with him, to get a sense of a day in the life. This doctor is a specialist in pain management. He is also a father and a slightly off-centre jazz musician. All in all, I would say that the hospital, and the people who work there, seem much more human and even fun than in the old days. Obviously, the staff take their work very seriously, but the mood on the unit is anything but grim.

This doctor was on his way to consult with a patient in another ward and so we walked through the labyrinth of construction at the Foothills, even getting lost a few times along the way. We eventually found his patient, who had come in with one issue but been found to have something else, much more serious. A complication. The doctor spent a very long time talking to this patient so he could design an effective pain management program.

On our way back to the unit, the doctor explained to me that many different pain medications can be used to alleviate suffering and help keep the patient as comfortable as possible. But then he added, "There's only one kind of pain we can't do anything about…and that's the pain of someone who ends up on our unit with no chance of recovery, and who realizes they haven't really lived their life…that's a pain that no one can take away from them."

Carpe diem, indeed.

FOR THE LAST few months, I've been spending time on the unit a little, getting to know some of the staff, and when possible visiting with the patients. I plan on doing this on an ongoing basis. I may have thought there was a book of poems or even a play in this experience, but now I'm not so sure. I'd like to think my motivation for these visits is more altruistic. If we see our lives in terms of narrative, it would be very sad indeed not to share that with someone. If I can be an audience for someone's story, then I feel my time and energy are being well spent.

I was visiting a patient last week, and knowing it would be my last visit before I wrote this piece, I asked if he would like me to share anything. He's a lovely man, and I know it may sound cliché, but I find visiting him a very humbling experience. He has such courage and even humour in the face of what is obviously a serious situation.

"It comes as a surprise," he said. "Your own death, it comes as a surprise. No matter how much time you have to get used to the idea, it still comes as a surprise." He talked about how the instinct to survive must surely be embedded in our DNA, and that the knowledge of our imminent death goes contrary to that instinct. In his mind, no matter how well you understand the situation intellectually, no matter how clearly your doctors lay it out for you, it always comes as a surprise.

Maybe that in part explains our denial of death and our tendency not to think about it. But when the time does come, as it will for us all, I take some comfort in knowing there are intelligent and compassionate people who will make the last part of our journey as pleasant as humanly possible.

Ideas under Glass

KATE TAYLOR

MANY INSTITUTIONS CAN lay claim to an uplifting foundation myth, but the new Canadian Museum for Human Rights boasts not one but two.

There is the story that Prime Minister Jean Chrétien was so moved by a visit to Auschwitz in 1999 that he declared a site would finally be found for a Canadian Holocaust museum.

There is also the anecdote told by Gail Asper, head of the family foundation that began the fundraising campaign for the museum and its chief advocate. The Asper Foundation regularly tours school groups to the United States Holocaust Memorial Museum and other sites in Washington DC and, on one of these trips, Asper found herself standing in line with her Canadian cohort waiting to see the American Declaration of Independence. Why, she wondered, was there nowhere in Canada where school children could see key documents in their country's human rights history.

A Canadian Holocaust memorial. An institution dedicated to human rights education. The first national museum outside Ottawa. The Canadian Museum for Human Rights slated to open sometime next year is a museum built on ideas.

And with what else would you build a museum? Well, with objects, actually.

The 19th-century museums that preceded today's institutions were treasure houses dedicated to the collection and preservation of wondrous things, great hordes of Old Master paintings and ivory tusks, Japanese fans and Paleozoic trilobites. In the 21st century we insist that these things must be organized to tell stories and if they mutely refuse we step in with text panels and video screens.

But as the story museum rises so too do ugly debates about whose version of events the museum's exhibitions must represent. The development of the CMHR has been marked throughout by an unseemly competition between the Jewish and Ukrainian communities over whose historic suffering will be given top billing. However exhibition space is finally distributed, the museum seems unlikely to satisfy all the competing agendas. Heedless of that lesson, the Canadian government has just opened up a whole second tier for debate with its decision to rename the Canadian Museum of Civilization in Gatineau, Quebec, the Canadian Museum of History, and to launch consultations as to what history this new institution should be telling. The glass display cases have been shattered and the museum wars rage on.

IF YOU WANT to remember what a museum used to feel like, visit the Redpath Museum at McGill University in Montreal, housed in the oldest purpose-built museum building in Canada. Renovations in 2003 have focused the exhibits in this Victorian charmer, but under its coffered ceiling, it still maintains some of the creative chaos bequeathed to it by geologist and McGill principal Sir William Dawson and his colleagues as they collected fossils, rocks, and Greek and Egyptian antiquities. It is one of those places where a dinosaur skeleton and a mummy case can happily sit side by side.

The sense that this is not good enough, that the public has neither the patience to read the small print nor the wit to place objects in context had become received wisdom by the 1970s. By the 1980s it was fashionable to point out that the supposedly neutral displays of objects actually contained their own prejudices and preconceptions. In 1989, the notorious *Into the Heart of Africa* exhibit at the Royal Ontario Museum in Toronto was an attempt to install in a new critical context the many African artifacts collected by Christian missionaries earlier in the century and left mouldering in the museum basement. With a bit of tongue in cheek, it attempted to depict 19th-century colonizing attitudes, but only succeeded in proving that museum audiences were completely unprepared for irony and that museum curators needed a lot more practice telling stories.

The major Canadian museum founded during this new narrative age was the Canadian Museum of Civilization, and it too was controversial from the start. The CMC has its roots in a collection of natural specimens and archeological and ethnographic material collected by the Geographical Survey of Canada in the 19th century. It had several homes and names before it became the bifurcated museums of Man and of Natural Sciences housed in the two wings of the Victoria Memorial Museum Building on Ottawa's Elgin Street. In the 1980s, the two institutions split and the half dedicated to the historical and ethnographic collections was given a nice, new gender-neutral name and a building of undulating sandstone designed by Métis architect Douglas Cardinal. Its soaring Grand Hall featuring the towering Pacific Coast aboriginal poles and colourful house fronts was from the start a smash hit, and remains a must-see for every foreign visitor to Ottawa.

The central history exhibit, on the other hand, was much criticized. Unveiled in sections throughout the 1990s, the Canada Hall takes the visitor from a 16th-century Basque whaling station on the Atlantic coast through 18th-century New France to a 19th-century Ontario main street and an early 20th-century ethnic bookstore in Winnipeg to a Vancouver airport in the 1960s. It has never been easy to distinguish what is an artifact and what is a replica in these carefully constructed displays where ephemeral pieces of social history that had long since rotted away – the Red River cart that carried meat and furs across the Prairies, for example – needed to be constructed from scratch. If the dioramas with their mannequins and sound effects now seem a tad quaint, in the 1990s they were perceived as an alarming new Disneyfication of the museum, turning a place that should have been dedicated to the judicious display of artifacts into a populist entertainment that made no distinction between the real and the reproduction. Nor did the clever way the hall covered a great swath of history and geography by following the continent's chronological settlement pattern from east to west please everyone: one Quebec columnist complained that a display that made no reference to her province after the days of New France implied Quebec was not a modern society. More recently, critics have lamented the lack of much reference to major political events such as the Riel Rebellion or the Acadian expulsion.

Despite criticisms, the Canada Hall has, in the end, proved highly popular with visitors who enjoy poking about the inside of an oil rig or a Victorian parlour, yet it is precisely this display that the museum is set to rethink, spurred on by a government that has picked the monarchy and the armed forces as its national icons and complains that nobody knows their Canadian history anymore. Education is, of course, a provincial jurisdiction, but perhaps a new Canadian museum of history would be a useful federal contribution, Heritage Minister James Moore speculated to the CBC when he announced the plan to rename the museum and grant $25 million toward a $30 million reworking of its history exhibits that will renovate almost a quarter of its floor space.

There are several red flags attached to the project: it certainly appears underfunded since it cost $50 million to build the original Canada Hall in the 1980s and '90s, in an age that did not demand the interactive, multimedia displays that contemporary visitors have come to expect. Although the minister has promised that the curators are to operate at arm's length, the museum cannot be blind to the government's interest in a kings-and-battles version of national history leading up to the 150th anniversary of Confederation in 2017, the date the exhibits are set to reopen.

In a gesture toward those who believe Canadian history is the celebration of Canadian achievements, the museum already added a hall of personalities in 2007, offering brief displays on 27 different figures who, to use the museum's own terms, inspired, founded, fought, built or governed, including writers Gabrielle Roy and Mordecai Richler and politicians Joey Smallwood and Jeanne Sauvé. Located on a mezzanine level above the Canada Hall, it not as popular with visitors as the quaint streets and shops below it: on a quiet weekend this winter, the Canada Hall was bustling with people while the figure of Sir John A. Macdonald stood forlornly at the start of his exhibit ready to give lessons in the Great Men and Women school of history to students who were nowhere in sight.

Canadians, when asked their opinions at consultations that the museum held last fall across the country, seem to prefer social to political history; or at least they are convinced that Canadian history is not simply the story of the powerful or famous. They also, of course, want to see their various ethnicities and communities represented; the Canada Hall already ticked off French, English, Ukrainian, Japanese, Chinese, African-Canadian and Filipino with its displays, but no doubt others will want in. Voices both inside and outside the aboriginal community have suggested that indigenous stories need to be included. This is somewhat ironic since the CMC's collection of indigenous objects is one of the best in the country, beautifully displayed in the Grand Hall and the galleries behind it. But it is stories, not artifacts, that are at issue in today's museum environment.

Nonetheless, the CMC's curators have not abandoned the search for telling objects. The museum has been beefing up its history collection in recent years and has just acquired a ceremonial last spike from the Canadian Pacific Railway, a strongbox that belonged to Sir John A's doctor and a large collection of objects retrieved from the *Empress of Ireland*, the CP ocean liner that sank in the St. Lawrence in 1914 in the worst maritime accident in the country's history.

At least the new Canadian Museum of History will have some artifacts to display.

The Museum for Human Rights is starting from scratch. Museum president Stuart Murray will not say what "iconic objects" the $350 million museum project might have acquired with the $37 million it is spending on the exhibits themselves. He mentions only the possibility that it will include a loan from Library and Archives Canada of the last letter written by Louis Riel before he was hanged, but he points out the museum's collection is mainly digital: it is collecting oral histories on such topics as women's rights, gay rights, aboriginal rights and the experiences of new Canadians. A spiral of glass erected at the historic Forks of the Red and Assiniboine rivers in downtown Winnipeg, the building, designed by U.S. architect Antoine Predock, will take visitors from a dark entry hall up toward the light. Its displays will cover notorious human rights abuses, including the Holocaust, the Ukrainian famine or Holodomor, and Canada's residential schools. But Murray stresses, "This is not a museum of human wrongs; it's a museum of human rights. It's not that you shy away from the disturbing material, but you look at it and say what happened, why and what can we learn from it."

This is programming a long way from the idea of a Holocaust museum originally bruited about when it was decided in the 1990s that the Canadian War Museum would not include a Holocaust gallery. In that instance, veterans had protested loudly, fearing that such a gallery would overshadow what they saw as their museum.

The question of whether the Jewish community will be satisfied with the much changed CMHR will only be answered on opening day, but the development process has featured a long and acrimonious debate about whether the Holocaust is a unique genocide that should be given the largest floor space in the new galleries. The new institution has done significant work with the Ukrainian community, which wishes to see the Holodomor given equal attention. It entered into a memorandum of understanding with Ukraine's Holodomor museum last year, has organized a series of lectures about the 1930s Stalinist state-sponsored famine in which millions died, and is commissioning a documentary film on the topic. However, the Ukrainian Canadian Congress still expresses reservations about the proposed exhibits, while the more radical Ukrainian Canadian Civil Liberties Association is actively protesting what it sees as an institution that will elevate one people's suffering over others. In a recent postcard campaign it denounced the CMHR as the pet project of a single community being unfairly underwritten by tax dollars.

In an article published last year in the *Journal of Genocide Research*, Australian scholar Dirk Moses identified the museum's dilemma, arguing that the CMHR was caught between its need to unite a multicultural Canada around a human rights agenda on the one hand and, on the other, the need to memorialize the tragedies of specific communities so as to meet its fundraising needs. Indeed, it is pinned between its two foundation myths, caught between Jean Chrétien's commitment to a memorial (which he later backed away from) and Gail Asper's vision of advocacy. The museum has raised $138 million from private donors to date, but Moses points out that communities who have made donations will feel they have bought space in this new institution. Murray is already dampening expectations, warning some communities they will not be represented on opening day, but promising that since the museum is primarily digital its exhibits will be ever changing. "If we tried to tell every story every community wanted us to tell we would never open this museum," Murray said.

Just as the federal government made its commitment to this difficult new national institution in 2007, it cancelled plans to build premises for a national portrait gallery that would house the large portrait collection of Library and Archives Canada. Both decisions seem largely political: the portrait gallery was an Ottawa initiative that had become associated with Liberal profligacy; the human rights museum was a Winnipeg project associated with Prime

Minister Stephen Harper's pro-Israel stance and with the decentralization of federal institutions. Still, they mark a telling choice to build a monument dedicated to complex ideas digitally displayed and call it a museum while a physical collection that languishes in storage can only represent itself to the public with digital images on a website.

"At the Holocaust Memorial Museum in Washington you round a corner and you see a bin of shoes. There is nothing you have to say," Murray observes. The thousands of shoes are on long-term loan from the Majdanek Museum at the site of the former Majdanek concentration camp in Poland. To buy such objects would seem horrible, to fabricate them worse still; and yet their presence is key to the story the Washington institution is telling and the display is often cited as visitors' most moving experience there. Sometime next year the doors will open in Winnipeg and a fractious, opinionated citizenry can judge whether the Canadian Museum for Human Rights has found its pile of shoes.

The Taste for Fiction: Rereading Novels, Reading the Self

RICHARD TELEKY

THE HEADLINE CAUGHT my eye: "Philip Roth Gives Up Reading Fiction." As I read on, the *New York Times* article cited an interview where Roth said, "I've stopped reading fiction. I don't read it at all. I read other things: History, biography. I don't have the same interest in fiction that I once did." When asked for an explanation, the novelist replied, "I don't know. I wised up…" and changed the subject. Regretfully, I knew what he meant.

For as long as I can remember I've been a devoted reader of fiction. One of my first loves was Anna Sewell's novel *Black Beauty* (1877), and as a boy I insisted on sleeping with a copy of it under my pillow. I didn't long for a horse, I wanted the book nearby. Ever since, I've been puzzled by people who didn't care for fiction, or who claimed they lacked the time for it. Even stranger were the people, always a few decades older than I, who said they had stopped reading novels: from my twenties, a Russian-born engineer who refused to read any novel longer than 200 pages, and in time not even those; from my thirties, a university librarian who gave away all her novels, except for *Don Quixote* and *The Hobbit*; and from my forties, an editor who lent me out-of-print novels by Henry Green – the last novels he had truly loved. What had gone wrong? This lack of interest in fiction, almost a distaste for it, would never happen to me.

Then decades passed. Gradually I picked up new fiction more from duty than interest. And for the first time in my reading life I found myself setting aside novels halfway through them. I continued to value fiction, and had even written three novels and a collection of short stories. Was I becoming detached from our culture, increasingly out of sympathy with it? Most of the pirouetting contemporary fiction by male writers – Martin Amis, Michael Chabon and Jeffrey Eugenides, for example – tried my patience, while novels by much-praised women writers such as Ann Patchett and Alice Sebold struck me as contrived or trite. I no longer wanted to read about alienated adolescents, impossible love affairs and messy marriages; postmodern effects were too clever by half; and the social commentary seemed like easy satire. Of course this wasn't true of every new novel I purchased – I loved Cynthia Ozick's *Heir to a Glimmering World*, Jill Clement's *Heroic Measures*, and Ward Just's *Forgetfulness* – but these were exceptions. Like Roth, I turned with greater pleasure to historical studies, biographies, memoirs, and journals. Could I recover a taste for fiction? I needed a plan. I needed to understand what was happening.

FICTION HAS MANY functions, which inevitably change over one's lifetime. We read novels and short stories to satisfy our curiosity about how others live as well as for entertainment, for comfort and consolation. Very few people, I suspect, read fiction mainly for the pleasures of language, though that shouldn't be discounted. Yet readers' interests evolve, and reading preferences may change along with them. Why, for instance, would anyone over sixty still *need* book after book about the love problems of fictional twentysomethings, a popular subject with writers and publishers? It's not that I want only novels about aging, but subject matter counts. As well, my work as a teacher determines some of my reading, and teaching classic novels has kept me close to books that have been favourites since I first discovered them. Rereading *Anna Karenina* or *To the Lighthouse*, for example (which stand up well to rereading) has also shaped my dissatisfaction with the thinness of most contemporary fiction.

The publishing, reviewing, and academic worlds distinguish between literary and popular fiction, a distinction both unavoidable and arbitrary. The popular nineteenth-century writer Charles Dickens would now be considered a classic or literary writer by most people. Other distinctions – such as "middlebrow," "bestseller" and "trash"– only suggest the trouble with categories. Grace Metalius's *Peyton Place* (1956), for example, once belonged to the categories of "bestseller" and "trash," but the novel is now available in paperback from the University Presses of New England, with a 24-page introduction that explains why it was considered shocking. Many books once thought to be literary (from 1957, James Gould Cozzens' turgid *By Love Possessed*) are now dismissed as middlebrow, and even pretentious. And it's amazing to recall that copies of a bestseller like Betty Smith's poignant *A Tree Grows in Brooklyn* (1943) were sent to American soldiers during the Second World War, because that novel has been relegated to the ghetto of books for teenage girls, who, as my students have told me, much prefer Stephenie Meyer's *Twilight* series about high-school vampires. Much of today's "literary" fiction is of no more value than once-praised novels that current writers and critics would dismiss. Reputations seesaw, but we like to overlook this fact and admire our own taste.

My plan to reinvigorate an appetite for fiction would begin with rereading, and I've now followed this plan for several years. Rereading involves the memories evoked by a book as well as the reflections that follow – a bit like looking through an old family album and rediscovering parts of one's self. In his essay "On Reading Old Books," published in 1821, William Hazlitt began his defence of rereading bluntly: "I hate to read new books. There are twenty or thirty volumes that I have read over and over again, and these are the only ones that I have any desire ever to read at all." It would be wrong to regard Hazlitt simply as an eccentric. A political radical with an interest in the English Romantic poets, he valued the satisfaction to be gained from books well known to him, and was glad to avoid having his "palate nauseated with the most insipid or vilest trash." Strong language, but Hazlitt was forty when he wrote his essay (not an old man for his era, but not a young one, either), which may help explain his stance. Age and experience can produce a sense of repetition – that one has seen "it" all before.

Closer to our own time, among the novelists who have written about rereading, both Larry McMurtry and Susan Sontag emphasized its importance as an act of understanding, with Sontag quipping, "Most of my reading is rereading." And John Irving has remarked, "When I love a novel I've read, I want to reread it – in part to see how it was constructed." The literary critic Patricia Meyer Spacks has even written an academic book about the subject, *On Rereading* (2011). All of them would likely agree with the critic Harold Bloom, who has argued that rereading is the only way to truly know a book. In the summer of 2009 a cluster of articles about rereading appeared. Verlyn Klinkenborg in the *New York Times* ("Some Thoughts on the Pleasures of Being a Re-Reader"), Roger Angell in the *New Yorker* ("Two

Emmas"), and David Gates in *Newsweek* ("Now, Read It Again") all wrote about it, and more recently David Bowman returned to it for the Book Review of the Sunday *New York Times* ("Read It Again, Sam"). One recurring idea was best expressed by Klinkenborg: "The characters remain the same, and the words never change, but the reader always does." It's this notion of change that intrigues me. Whether from curiosity or for escape or nostalgia, we reread in the shadow of memory, which may be part of the pleasure. Who were we? Who are we? Meyer Spacks suggests that rereading can seem like an indulgence because most people have limited time and there's always an unread book waiting. I'm not convinced by her argument. Reading can never be exhaustive as long as people keep writing. As we reread, we have to look at ourselves more closely.

The books of one's teenage years vary from one generation to another and shape reading habits for years to come. From the seventh grade on, when I read my mother's copies of John O'Hara's *From the Terrace* and *A Rage to Live*, I longed to be an adult, with the freedom to go to the theatre, enjoy martinis, and have an adulterous affair – though I wasn't quite sure why. And I may have belonged to the last generation of young North Americans to carry around thick copies of Russian novels. Somehow we knew that these were the books we *should* be reading, books that belonged to the Western canon before it came to be regarded as oppressive rather than liberating. Where did our idea – a kind of aspiration – come from? As a teenager I had part-time jobs as a library page, first in my high school and then in the local library, and as books passed through my hands, one after another tempted me. I recall this instance vividly: after watching a Hollywood version of *The Brothers Karamazov* in the ninth grade, I borrowed the library's copy and convinced myself that my family resembled the Karamazovs because my maternal grandfather reminded me of Lee J. Cobb as the movie's difficult Papa K. This was unfair to both Dostoevsky and to my grandfather, but that didn't matter then because I *needed* to measure my own experience against the books I read.

Fiction's capacity to take readers back in time may explain the teenage taste I had for novels by Thomas B. Costain (*The Black Rose*, 1945), Anya Seton (*The Winthrop Woman*, 1958), Margaret Mitchell (*Gone with the Wind*, 1936), and Irving Stone (*Lust for Life*, 1934), once all bestsellers. Their dull, flat prose now surprises me, but these writers could tell stories. The years that followed led me to prefer Marco Polo's *Travels* to Costain, John Winthrop's *Journals* to Seton's bodice-ripper, Mary Chesnut's Civil War *Diary* to Mitchell's romantic saga, and Van Gogh's letters to Stone's bio-novel. Growing up explains a lot – growing up and away from the dominant culture's bestsellers. Still, I remember the sense of discovery these novels once gave me; the fact that they were library books endowed them with a kind of stature. But why should I now care for Kathryn Harrison's novel *Enchantments*, about Rasputin's daughter? One day Harrison will take her place beside Costain and Seton. Historical romances are substitutes for the real thing. Of course great writers have set novels in the past – Tolstoy's *War and Peace* (1868) and Lampedusa's *The Leopard* (1958) come to mind – but they weren't using the past to justify colourful adventure or to piggy-back on a historical figure. And they were both great writers.

It's fascinating to thumb through *Books of the Century: A Hundred Years of Authors, Ideas and Literature* (1998), edited by Charles McGrath, which contains reviews culled from the *New York Times*. While there's an emphasis on books that have lasted, reviews of some now-forgotten novels did make it into the 600-page tome – for instance, Herman Wouk's 1955 bestseller, *Marjorie Morningstar*, which *almost* survives a reread. In his 1956 review of it, Maxwell Geismar concluded with a sniff: "*Marjorie Morningstar* is very good reading indeed. But to this reviewer at least, the values of true culture are as remote from its polished orbit as are, at base, the impulses of real life." *True culture?* Today I can guess at his meaning, but not at fifteen. Even better than McGrath, the critic Jonathan Yardley has examined his reading life in *Second Readings: Notable and Neglected Books Revisited* (2011). His book strikes me as serious and apt, which means that we probably share some common values and tastes. Yardley finds much to admire in Daphne du Maurier's *Rebecca*, whose "sales would be envied by many a Flavor of the Month author of ostensibly 'serious' fiction." Wisely, he admits that "one of the built-in liabilities of doing a series of literary reconsiderations is that it exposes one's treasured youthful tastes to the cold light of a more mature reading." Rereading can be humbling.

Many of the books I once enjoyed were no better than the contemporary novels I easily set aside. My taste and standards, however, have been shaped by half a century of reading. And Sontag, McMurtry, Roth, and Meyer Spacks also had decades of reading under their belts. Age probably accounts for some of the impatience I share with Roth, because a growing sense of mortality does make a difference in what a reader wants from a book, and the consciousness of less time ahead contributes to a shift in taste. One wonders how real people, rather than fictional characters, face the end of their lives: biographies and memoirs, after all, are just obituaries writ large. It's no surprise that much contemporary fiction echoes a novelistic tradition that for centuries has thrived on the twists and turns of a love story. But the search for love – its richness and disappointments – tells me, with each passing year, less and less that I still *need* to know.

In the spring of 2012, when the Pulitzer Prize committee declined to offer an award for the best novel of the past year, Ann Patchett, who had published a book that some reviewers considered a contender, wrote an op-ed piece for the *New York Times*. In it she took the high road: "Let me underscore the obvious here: Reading fiction is important. It is a vital means of imagining a life other than our own, which in turn makes us more empathetic beings." If only it were true. I've known many fiction readers – and writers – who are *un*empathetic to say the least, and my experience surely isn't unique. There's a self-serving edge to Patchett's remarks ("Buy my book," she implies, "and you'll be a better person") that troubles me. According to her logic, fiction suits mainly the very young. If a person hasn't learned empathy by the age of forty, it's probably too late. Think of Cervantes, Balzac, Dickens and Tolstoy: if their novels haven't made better people of us, there's little reason to expect much from new fiction writers. Patchett's touching notion is reduced to a sweet platitude by any daily newspaper.

ALTHOUGH MY PLAN to spark a new taste for fiction wasn't a complete success, perhaps I'm an optimist, at least when it comes to books. I just purchased a copy of the English translation of Herta Müller's novel *The Hunger Angel*. Born in 1953, Müller won the Nobel Prize for literature in 2009. Why not give her a chance? The book sits on my bedside table and I eye it with some trepidation. I *want* to like it. Müller's own story – her girlhood in Romania herding cows, her life in a German-speaking minority under Nicolae Ceausescu's dictatorship, and the fact that she wrote herself into another life – makes me wish *The Hunger Angel* was a memoir. But it's not, it's a novel. Okay. I reach for it. Maybe this time.

Year Zero

DANIEL SCOTT TYSDAL

I WAS EXPECTING a different package. On Sunday, I had ordered an exceptionally rare Cambodian comic book, paying the online seller 25 bucks extra for next day delivery. Still comic-less four days later, I went to bed certain I'd been scammed. So this morning, when I finally realized it was not the theme song for some 8-bit fantasy-adventure game steering me out of sleep, or the mating call of a low-end android, but, in fact, my landline chiming one last time as someone from outside tried and failed to buzz up, I threw on a housecoat and hurried to the lobby to catch the UPS delivery guy before he, and my Khmer Rouge-era comic, got away.

At ground level, though, no UPS employee peered through the frosted glass, no van darted into the slushy rush hour traffic on King Street West. A middle-aged woman, plump with layers, shivered in the late December cold, holding her white cane to her chest and clutching her hijab tight against the bursts of wind-powdered snow. The cabbie, who the woman had dragged out of the heated car to help her, rubbed his sweatered arms for warmth as he flashed his urgent glance from his idling taxi to his blind customer and then to the condo's directory, trying to determine if he had punched the wrong code. The woman's last name was Ahmed. I don't remember her first name. I only met her once, at her daughter's funeral, but I recognized her as soon as I saw her face.

She had the same lips as Najwan, the bottom much plumper than the top, and, like Najwan, the corners of her mouth dropped so severely when she was distraught that it warped into the shape of a boomerang or banana what could be, when still, a very elegant mouth. Mrs. Ahmed had the same high cheekbones and narrow chin as her daughter, too, though these features had been rounded by years, swollen slightly, as though she were Najwan, post-bee sting, or as though Najwan and I had both been zapped by a shrink ray and I was seeing her through the distorting curve of a giant, water-filled glass.

The cabbie caught me watching from the foyer and gave a hopeful wave. I had to fight the urge to ride the elevator back up to the safety of my concrete burrow. Mrs. Ahmed lived north of where I taught, the University of Toronto Scarborough, so I knew her visit was urgent – the ride downtown having set her back at least 100 bucks. The cabbie added a pleading smile to the waving of his exposed hand. The smile I tried to return died quickly. I didn't have the energy to pretend. Any stab I took at faking faltered at the thought of all the different storms this woman could unleash. The dread was palpable. My intestines threatened to freefall, to make themselves a fleshy rope that knotted further my already immobile feet. The cabbie finally gave up on me and alerted his fare to my presence.

"Professor Tysdal?" Najwan's mother ventured, her words muted by the glass.

"Yes," I said, and then, leaning out the door, continued, "Mrs. Ahmed. How are you?"

"Freezing," she said, her words inflected with her Pakistani lilt, "but very pleased you remember me."

"Of course I remember you," I said, "I've been meaning to get in touch."

"Your time is valuable, Professor. I expected you had many big responsibilities."

"But I promised to. At the funeral. To see if I could answer any questions you might have."

"Perhaps we could talk inside?"

"Yes, sorry. Please come in."

I tempered my invitation upstairs with a comment about the disorder of my loft. She graciously declined my offer, adding that she did not want to waste my valuable time. I was so on edge that a part of me wondered if she kept referring to my time as "valuable" because she knew I planned to waste the day watching a few episodes of the 1963 season of *The Outer Limits*, *The Twilight Zone* knockoff I had picked up for myself on Blu-ray for Christmas. She asked the driver to wait, and then agreed with him that, yes, it would be best for him to return to his car and restart the meter. She knew business was always tight. Her husband had driven taxi.

As the cabbie scampered back into the cold, Mrs. Ahmed confessed that she was pressed for time herself. She had to get back home to meet her sister and sister-in-law. They were helping her clean out Najwan's bedroom. Two years later, they had finally talked her into moving her daughter's things into storage, the compromise they had settled on when she refused to sell Najwan's possessions or throw them out.

"That is why I have come to visit you by surprise," she said, leaning her cane against her hip and reaching into her bag, "while we were cleaning, we found this."

She withdrew a sealed 10 x 15 catalogue envelope. The envelope was addressed to me. It was so stuffed that Mrs. Ahmed needed both hands to hold it out for me to take.

"This is for you," she said, extending the envelope even further into the space between us.

"I'd better not," I said, "if Najwan had wanted me to have it she would have mailed it."

"Maybe she never had the chance."

"You and your family have the right to keep anything your daughter left behind."

"I insist."

"Really, I can't."

"Please!"

Her voice broke. She pushed the envelope so far forward that she had to take a step to keep her balance, sending her cane to the floor with a crack. I knelt quickly and retrieved it. She took the cane from me. I caught the envelope as she let it drop into my hands.

The cramped printing was Najwan's. The letters of my name and of my home address were inked so closely together that they looked like everlasting intimates, or inmates coerced to subsist in close quarters. I recognized her writing from the work she had submitted in my "Creating Comics" course and the yellow sticky notes she left on my office door, "I hope you're having a great day, sir," or "Just dropped by to say hi, sir," crowded into the word balloons that emerged from the mouths of the amphibial, insect-like creatures she loved to invent.

I looked up at Mrs. Ahmed. Muddy bags much darker than her auburn skin encircled her eyes. When she had handed me the package, one of the straps of her purse had slipped off her shoulder, and, as I watched her stare emptily at a space just above my forehead, I eyed that opening.

If I was careful, I could slip the envelope back into her purse without her knowing.

"It was in with some things a friend of Najwan's returned after the funeral," she said, breaking our silence, and, perhaps sensing my scheme, pulling the strap of her purse back over her shoulder. "My brother's wife found it. Luckily, she made the mistake of asking me about it before tearing it open. My sister had to drive her home because she refused to stop whining, 'What's inside? What's inside?' That is why I regretfully had to disturb you so early this morning. I wanted to give you the envelope before she brought my brother. He would have made me do it without your permission."

Hopeful, I took this as a cue. Maybe she really wanted to keep the contents of the envelope, but her honesty prevented it. She believed she had to give me the right of first refusal.

"You've done your duty," I said, "now let's have a look together."

"I don't want to know what is in there."

"I don't mind."

"I don't want to know."

Her hand reached out, paddling in the air, until the fingers of her winter-chilled gloves found my fingers and stilled them against the envelope.

"No matter what people wrote about my family," she said, her eyes welling up, "we loved our Najwan, and we always – always – tried to do what was best for her. She trusted you. I know this. And if she trusted you, I trust you. I give you what is yours."

She turned suddenly to leave, the hard end of her cane striking the tile, then the door, with a sharp click. I reached out to help her to the cab, but she brushed my hand aside.

"I promise to call if it's anything important," I said.

"Call me if it brings you peace, Professor. Only then. Peace is the one thing I need."

IN THE ELEVATOR, I hit P2 instead of going straight up to my place on the fifth floor, the envelope pinned between my torso and my arm like a stolen painting. It was the wrong painting, though. That was the thief I felt like. With no fence to free me from my illicit spoils, I had to make a decision. Destroy the thing? Break back into the gallery and return the work to its spot on the wall? Or hang it in my home, learn to appreciate the aesthetic and technical properties of what I had only seen before as property to pinch?

The parking level storage room was a collection of interconnected cages that stood six feet high. Some of the cages were empty except for a few weeping cans of interior paints with names like "Roman Ruins," "Lemon Tart," and "Samba." Another cage contained only a framed velvet canvas that tackily preserved the wide eyes, pointy breasts, and almond skin of a local's take on a tourist's vision of a foreign nation's fairer sex. Another was packed with the ghosts of recreations past – golf clubs, tennis racquets, croquet mallets, snorkel gear – while another confined "the replaced" – the replaced microwave, the replaced mini-fridge, the replaced speakers and amp. This was the storage space as holding cell, the final stop before disposal.

The overhead fluorescent lights, for reasons that remain unclear clear to me, were also caged, further restraining their weak glow and making it hard for me to distinguish the storage space key from the rest of my tiny keys: mail key, desk key, the key to a bike lock that was bolt-cuttered to bits by some crook three summers past. It was somewhere behind the junk that filled my cage that I buried it, the box of Najwan's things, the things I saved. I don't mean her personal effects, just the items you would expect a professor to possess: my copies of her old assignments, the hardcopies I had made of our email correspondence (for when Gmail eventually went under), and clippings of the articles written after her life was taken, some in languages other than English. The story of her death had gone global for a few days. Then it was done. "No legs," as they say. That is all.

I unlocked the cage, placed the envelope on top, and got to work pulling out item after item: suitcases, a dolly with a wonky wheel, mismatched lamps, the full-body Predator costume I had blown a fortune on but never ended up wearing for Halloween because the helmet made me claustrophobic. Normally, I took comfort in the thick, sweet scent of old exhaust that permeated the parking levels. It's the complexity of the odour that is so attractive, the way it signals travel and home, departure and return. Plus, I grew up on a farm so I associate the smell of gas, and diesel, and the lawnmower's mix of petrol and oil, with nature, with the earth. It brought to mind the upside-down ocean of a blue sky that crests a field's green, then golden, and then harvested growth. It reminded me of the light that bursts in sharp beams through the holes in the barn's tin wall, undertaking in the dark the sort of luminous archaeology that makes petrified claws and trilobites and spearheads of all the airborne dust. This morning, though, the stink of the parking garage simply inspired nausea. It worked in cahoots with Mrs. Ahmed's intrusion, the envelope, and my empty stomach to leave me feeling seven-years-old-and-three-hours-on-the-merry-go-round ill. Oddly enough, this feeling gave me an idea for my superhero strip, *The Swipe*. These ideas still came to me intermittently, even though I had quit drawing

The Swipe three years back. The Swipe is strapped into a madman's amusement park ride, some sort of "beyond the pleasure principle" Gravitron. He is about to be spun into mush when he gets a whiff of it, this stink of exhaust that is the residue of the killing machine's fuel, the residue of what the terminal ride had burned to wipe out those it had wiped out before him.

I finally freed up the 3 × 3 stack of BCW comic boxes that stretched to the back of the cage, the boxes that protected the comics I had devoured when I was a kid and the collections I had ordered online since but had not gotten around yet to reading. Three rows in I reached the box that contained Najwan's things, which I had simply marked "Naj." I lifted the lid enough to stuff the envelope inside. I shut the lid tight, and then reburied that box behind the comics, the costume, lamps, luggage, and dolly, though I would have preferred to use concrete or fast-hardening molten steel to stop me from ever returning to dig back in.

DO YOU GET rattled? I mean, when something shakes you, do you stay shaken? If you're like me, there is this sort of sub-body within your body that vibrates intensely after you have been disturbed or threatened or exposed or outright attacked, buzzing like a pipe saw on its way through an endless inch of alloy steel and drowning out even the most well-composed orchestra of equanimity and reason. This body, a mishmash of sensation and fantasy and sentiment and reality, invisible to everyone outside you, yearns to take the controls of your flesh and bone body, to become known. It wants to captain a weeklong bender whose spoils are a mysterious softball-sized lump on the side of your face and the contraction of a venereal disease. Or it wants to shut your engines right down, impound you in bed and release you only for bathroom breaks and to hastily refuel on un-nuked microwave pizzas.

Returning from the storage room in the parking garage, I could feel this body birthing beneath my skin, maturing rapidly from the baby-sized ball of sickness in my gut to a full-fledged nervous system-distending force with a voice that urged, "Go get the envelope. Go get the envelope." A headache was coming on, too, one of those caffeine withdrawal doozies that simulate an ice pick lobotomy. I made a quick cup of instant coffee to keep it in check. Fresh mug in hand, I took a seat on the toilet on the main floor, pants at my ankles even though I had no urge to go. It was a preventative gesture, like the wolf man who cuffs himself in a cage before every full moon. How much life-altering damage had been done by men seated on the can? I mean, historically speaking. I took a big swig of coffee, chewed and swallowed the crystals that had not dissolved in the lukewarm water, and caught a glimpse of myself from the nose up in the bathroom mirror. Maintaining firm but sympathetic eye contact, I mentally broke the situation down for my reflection in the simplest terms possible.

After this semester, the 12-week term that was set to begin in ten days, I will have the summer to prepare and submit my promotion dossier. Forgetting the envelope equals committing to my present success equals a secure job at UTSC for the rest of my life. Obsessing over the envelope equals falling back into past failures equals (at the age of thirty-five) heading back to Starbucks or Chapters or Philthy McNasty's and fighting to publish indie comics that do not attract enough readers to keep a roof over my head and, if I am lucky, win me accolades that pay even less.

My reflection in the mirror cut my anxiety-riddled counsel short.

"Sell-out," it spit.

I flinched, but did not look away.

"Quitter," my reflection sneered, "you fake."

I stood up from the toilet to confront its abuse, its accusation, its mantra, "Sell-out, quitter, fake. Sell-out, quitter, fake." As I brought my face closer to the mirror, the intensity of my reflection's attack increased, the volume and the speed of its chanted charge, until I was so intimate with its barely audible shriek that the material reflected in the glass looked less like the features of a face and more like a heap of dough beaten by an invisible Mixmaster. It was like some sort of un-felicitous calculus was being performed in my unconscious: if X does not open the envelope and let it differentiate X into pieces, then Y will massacre the coordinates in which the envelope and X exist. There was this mad chimp inside me with a machine gun and mallet who wanted to be let loose in the maternity ward of my future kin. I charged out of the bathroom and made another cup of coffee, this time waiting until the kettle squealed. I was that other werewolf, the one who controlled the lunar cycle and was this close to shouting to the full moon, "Rise!"

I decided to give the beast a little freedom in my office, the north facing room on the second floor of my loft. Even with this mere sliver of control, the beast felt a sick joy at the thought of tossing my computer through the window and filling my home with the blizzard that erased from view the roofs of townhouses, the roofs of old houses not yet levelled to make room for more townhouses, and, beyond that, the denuded branches of the tallest trees in Trinity Bellwoods Park, which, if the beast could have seen them, would have looked to it like the skeletons of mushroom clouds. My hope was to quell the urge for the envelope with some virtual marauding. The beast started by sending a noxious email to the seller in L.A. who failed to deliver my Cambodian comic book, including with the invective multiple links to the definition of the phrase "next day delivery." The beast then took on the students who – in their timeless quest for an easy elective – had written me to request syllabi for the Winter term. Rather than admitting to them that nothing had yet been finalized, the beast composed epic syllabi characterized by ten thousand page reading lists, multi-lingual assignments, and three hour presentations performed in groups of fifty. The beast visited the discussion forums of indie comic sites, and, finding the rare thread that discussed my work, attacked my attackers and gave my defenders hell.

The e-ssault was not enough. The manic urge to rip the envelope open remained, the urge to retrieve the envelope and let whatever it contained rip me open. Those emails were the equivalent of trying to quench a baby Gargantua's thirst for the milk of 17,913 cows with a Slim-Fast 3-2-1 Plan, Low Carb Diet Ready-to-Drink Shake. I paced my office, coughing so hard I would have vomited if I had anything more than coffee to throw up. I paced more, expanding my route to include my bedroom, the stairwell, and then the main floor, where I grabbed a carton of milk to subdue the burning acidity of the java. As my coughing worsened, transforming into a genuine dry heave, I started to wonder if I had eaten the envelope. Was my memory of caging the envelope in the supply room a screen for what I had really done? What if I had actually swallowed the envelope bite by bite to consume and dispose of it in one efficient act? The thought turned my stomach that final, fateful notch, and I darted back into the can and buried my barking head in the bowl. Not a single shred of envelope floated in the milky mess I ejected.

I turned to *The Outer Limits* for salvation. I sought liberation through numbness, freedom through immersion in cultural swill. The four episodes on the first disc barely held me. I continued to fidget. I got up to send apology emails to my students, admitting that the baroque syllabi were a bad joke I liked to play on such industrious pupils. I ordered pizza from 3-4-1. I closed, opened, and re-closed the curtains over the windows on the main and second floor, shutting out the blizzard that had let up but still resembled the frozen locust plague sent by a miserable bunch of frozen gods. I endured in my quest for sanctuary in *The Outer Limits*, though, and halfway through the second disc it worked. I was the drunk who wanted to forget the terrible mistakes of his parents, and to forget the terrible mistakes he had made trying to forget the terrible mistakes of his parents, by consuming drink after drink. I consumed episode after episode and I was soon soothed by the black and white images, the hacky storytelling, the rumbling cymbal of the theme song, and the Control Voice in the voiceover warning at the start of each episode that they controlled this transmission, they controlled the sharpness of the image, they controlled the horizontal and the vertical of my television set. It was comforting, that feeling of nostalgia, of nostalgia for a very specific nostalgia that could never be mine. I felt like I had plopped down into one of the hammocks dads used to tie between trees in one-panel comics and family comedies. I was secure in this longing to feel lonesome for a time I was never, and could never be, an exile from.

By the fourth disc, I transcended that feeling, transcended feeling, really, achieving a kind of tele-medial singularity, unmediated emersion, the viewing equivalent of the pugilist's punch drunk, *dementia screenistica*. This was the true real, the real truth, the pain and doom and fury of these aliens and outsiders and technologies and monsters: the scientist who is transformed into an alien to unite world powers against a common enemy and end the Cold War, the professor whose unconscious takes charge of his mind-control implant and commits unspeakable acts, the time travelling mutant who returns to our era to stop the human-made plague that deformed him, the Martians who visit earth to study humankind's peculiar penchant for murder. Reality was a ruse. The twittering of tree-concealed sparrows, the kitchen thick with the aroma of roasting garlic, the visible bursts of breath as one friend stilled in the cold confides in her most vital companion, the sublime gap that yawns between ascending airplanes hitting their ceilings and the deepest depths of the ocean floor, the hypnotic patterns of skin cells and arabesque wallpaper, the mingling shadows of escalator-bound commuters cast by the sinking sun on the train station's far wall – all of these details were designed, or devised, or evolved to conceal the total reality of this very program. *Life* is the mere episode. *These episodes* are Life. The one good act, the only good life, was to reproduce these residents of the outer limits, to witness them, to let them totally occupy your consciousness, to take control as the Control Voice said, until you could sincerely hail each creature's demand to "take me to your leader" with the reply, "I take you to yourself. You are it."

I HAVE WRITTEN to you before, though you have not read what I wrote for you. And you won't read it. That was the first thing I did when I woke on my couch just after 1 a.m. Friday morning, the Blu-ray's home screen composed of a collage of black and white, rubber horrors and looping the first 20 seconds of *The Outer Limits'* theme song. I came up here to my office, sat down at my computer, and moved the folder titled, "After Naj," to the Trash. "You cannot undo this action," I was warned when I hit, "Empty." It is permanent. This emptying. Emptying actions cannot be undone. I clicked, "OK," and deleted forever the draft outline for my book about Najwan, along with the handful of paragraphs I had saved following my most recent purge, eight months back.

I created a new folder and named it, "After Envelope." I opened a blank document and I started to write to you. I wrote about Mrs. Ahmed's surprise visit. I wrote about storing Najwan's unsent envelope in the basement. I wrote about having a meltdown instead of opening the envelope. And now I write this, 2:43 a.m. Saturday morning, a little over 24 hours after starting. I write this sentence that tells you I have not retrieved the envelope from storage. I write this sentence to let you know that I wrote and write all of this for you. Whoever you are, reader, consumer, witness, you have been with me since Najwan died. No, that's a lie. You were with me well before that, quite intensely, but after she died you changed. Or what I wanted to say to you changed. Or what I had to say to you. How I had to say it.

What's in the envelope? My hope is that it contains more of what I already saved, more of what I know, more of Najwan's comics, more of her essays, maybe something a tad more personal, like a journal, though I can't imagine her being any more open than she was in her work, or, for that matter, in her posts on Facebook and Blogger and deviantArt. I know from chatting with her that she wrote more comics than I have read. She liked drawing these collections of disconnected four-panel strips that depicted the spectrum of a personal relationship, with her parents, for example, or her siblings, her artistic heroes, her religion.

She did a piece on her mom's blindness. There was a strip about her older sister who, grounded, rearranged the furniture to thwart their mom's mental map of their home. There was a strip about Najwan not really getting what it meant that her mom was blind until she witnessed the reaction of her kindergarten classmates. In the most powerful strip, she asks her mom if she regretted being blind. Her mom said, "no," she had a rich life, and, she was certain, a good enough grasp of most things sight-based, including faces, dimensions, and colour, though she did confess that she wished she knew what people meant when they talked about different "shades."

What do you think is in the envelope? Would you share? If I drew four blank panels on this page, would you draw what you thought? If you have a bunch of different theories, draw them all. Divide the panels into as many pieces as you've got ideas. Or if you're one for suspense, you could depict the moment I tear the envelope open, zooming in panel by panel, and ending so close in the last panel that no one can discern what I withdraw. Or zoom out, so that in the last panel the viewer is positioned far above the city, seeing things from an impossible point in the sky, my window an unshaded dot lost in a galaxy of unshaded dots.

Or perhaps I am asking the wrong thing. What *is* the envelope? Maybe that is the real question. What sort of story will unfold from the origin of its opening? What sort of hero will emerge? The envelope could be the alien child crash landing on earth after his parents rocketed him free from an exploding planet. The envelope could be the radioactive spider that bites an unsuspecting hand. The envelope could be the bat that bursts through the mansion window, inspiring the orphan to choose chiropteric features to form his new, crime-fighting identity.

I don't mean to delay or to be a tease. I really don't know what is in the envelope. And I don't want to know, not yet, anyway. Whatever she sent me will force me to confront my failure, even if the envelope contains nothing more than blank pages, or the book I wrote and published in an alternate dimension Najwan miraculously visited and returned from. I will open the envelope in the morning, a time you can reach quickly by passing your eyes over the blank space that follows these words, but a moment that I hope will be delayed for me by a night of time-transcending dreams, or a peaceful sleep, at least, free of visions like the one I had while napping this afternoon, the lone break I took from writing to you. A leech had attached itself to my chest, right above my heart. I could not tear it off with my hands or slice it off with my knife. I tried my lighter, in an attempt to heat the leech into letting go, but its skin caught fire, and my skin caught, too, and that slick green thing remained stuck to me as we both went up in flames.

THE ENVELOPE CONTAINS two items: a notebook and a card.

The notebook – a Mead Five Star three-subject wirebound notebook, to be more specific – belonged to one of my colleagues at UTSC, Dr. Thomas Buchanan Merrow. The words "Mead" and "Five Star" are worn to a faint silver dust on the black plastic cover. Tom, a scholar of 20th-century American literature from Montana, made his first entry in the notebook in the spring of 2010. The cardboard back of the notebook, half-torn off the wire rings, is veined with lines where the cardboard cracked and folded. In some unknown moment of boredom, Tom traced these lines over in black ink, bringing them into further relief, so that they resemble the seams of a valuable mineral riveleting a

cave's stony terrain, or the flashing forks of a quiver of lightning bolts halted in their most Zeus-thrown form. I have
only had the chance to flip through the notebook. A simple
journal seems to have been its initial purpose. However, as
Tom's obsession with Najwan grew, the notebook also grew,
becoming a storehouse for all things Najwan: a scrapbook
for mementos, an archive for her marks and remarks, a testing ground for the book Tom had started to write about her.

The card included in the envelope with the notebook is
from Najwan. She made the card herself from a piece of A4
Bristol board folded in half. The front of the card is wordless,
decorated only with one of Najwan's cryptids, a sickle-tailed
one-eyed creature with the wings of a bat and a tiny, fanged
mouth that, opened wide, is about 1/10th the size of the eye.
Speed lines suggest the creature is about to fly off the edge
of the card and escape into whatever awaits it in the world
beyond the card's undecorated border. Inside the card,
Najwan wrote me a short note. "As you probably already
know, sir," she began, "I have to leave Toronto." She thanked
me for all my help, and then she asked me for one last favour.
She hated to trouble me, after all I had already done, but she
was hoping I could return the enclosed notebook to Professor Merrow. "You will be rewarded," she finished, "with
72 black-eyed virgins in paradise (Jokes! ☺)." She signed
the card, "Your grateful student always, Naj." The card was
dated, Wednesday, December 1st, 2010. That was the day
before she was attacked, four days before she died.

There is a story that needs to be told. I had always
thought that someone else would tell it. I was absolutely
certain the facts of Najwan's death would spread to artists
of every ilk – creative non-fiction activists, sober novelists,
splatterers of house paints on massive canvases, Hollywood producers with major pull, cynical minimalist poets,

guerrilla graffitist, post-country but pre-robotronic steel guitarists, YouTube curators, the composer of mainstream operatic opuses, and on and on and on. And these vast acres of creators would be unable to resist the seed of insight into total injustice that Najwan's story spread, the seed of a feeling of hope spurred at the thought of the woman and the world that could have been. And these artists would nourish work that exposed the Dark Age we had been cast into when this bright star was snuffed out, art that stoked a palace coup of the Ruling Absolute (Love over Hate! Hope over Fear! Fellow Feeling over Solipsistic Greed!), voices that inspired an end to apathy and acquiescence, crying to us, "Welcome life! Encounter for the first time the fragile multiplicity of experience, and re-script in the code of your spirit the buggy conscience of our kind."

It was more than mourning. When she died, I swelled. I transformed. What was once just a man exploded suddenly into miles and miles and miles of Stone Age terrain, miles of Lower Palaeolithic expanses scorched in a time of blight, darkened in a time of an inviolably eclipsed sun. Yet, within this pre-ancient wasteland one hominid endured, stoking a fire at the mouth of a cave, bearing this flame into the wild on branches in his quest to find others who would also preserve and spread this warmth and illumination. And following Najwan's initial bloom in the rushed and artless doggerel of news agency hacks and Botoxed talking heads, I waited for the first signs of revolution. My assumption at the time was that the upheaval would start with requests for interviews from serious journalists, or from popular sensationalists and socially conscious academics. I waited for those first responders to arrive. I was ready to help them resuscitate the fading story, to give them whatever material they needed to compose the initial, world-changing work, whether that work be an overly sensational "true crime" exposé with a hokey, pun-packed title (for example, *A Veiled Truth*), or a more academic offering with an even hokier long-winded subtitle, like *Thomas Buchanan Merrow, Honour Killed, and the Dark Side of the Western University*.

These journalists never came. No one did. The high point has remained the story published in *The Toronto Star* a week after Najwan died in hospital. A former UTSC student, who had been interning with the *Star*'s Entertainment Section, wrote the piece, "How the Plan to Save Najwan Ahmed Failed." Her connections to the school gave the student a decent insight into the mechanics of what happened, but she failed to capture any of the story's real significance. For all the wrong reasons, it was the picture of Najwan that accompanied the article that caused a stir. The former student had snuck into Najwan's hospital room, against the family's wishes, to take the picture of Najwan on her deathbed, and a public debate ensued about journalistic ethics. The student was attacked for callous exploitation. She was defended for upholding her right to preserve good old-fashioned facts.

Maybe this picture of Najwan had too many layers for people to really see it. There were the layers of the coma and life-sustaining machines that concealed her vibrancy and silliness and sadness and cunning. There were the layers of blankets covering a body misshapen by a beating that broke bones and ruptured organs. The layers of bandages wrapped around her head concealed the face a jar of sulphuric acid had scorched, erased completely, one eye destroyed for sure and the nose and lips effaced of shape and sense and tone. Death was a layer, too. It hid forever the future in which Najwan's face healed into the smooth, featureless features of that appalling sorority of acid-attack victims, the future in which she stared into us with wide-eyed desperation, pleading, "No more, never again," from behind a visage that appeared so mask-like, even though it was really the opposite of a mask, the universal root of every particular human face, the base face desired by and achieved through the basest hate.

After *The Star* article, the web publication of Najwan's comics was the only other initiative worth noting. I started a blog and posted scanned copies of her work, both the autobiographical stuff and her weirder, creature-filled comic strip fables. The strip titled, "The Children," from which the one-eyed cryptid on the card in the envelope originates, was the biggest success. The story begins in 1915 with the children from an unnamed village in an unnamed country being conscripted to participate in the Great War. The parents are promised that the children will not see action. Instead, they will serve as scouts on the borders of friendly cities, keeping an eye out for saboteurs. A new threat soon overtakes the village's anxieties about the war when they come under attack by a sickle-tailed, one-eyed flying monster. The creature kills adult after adult, driving its hooked tail into the stomachs of its victims, and with a hide impervious to bullet or blade the thing seems unstoppable. A number of villagers admit feeling thankful for the war. Against this monster, their children would not have stood a chance. Twenty villagers are brutally disembowelled before the monster is finally trapped in a barn, and the barn is burned to the ground. Soon after this victory, the war ends and the villagers receive the good news that their children will be returning home, with all of them having survived except for one who went AWOL. The next morning, the military train pulls into the station to the applause of the villagers. The applause quickly die, though, as soldiers bearing cages, not the children, exit the train. The comic ends with the soldiers opening the cages and setting the children free. They emerge, one-eyed and sickle-tailed, wings flapping, permanently bound to the shape the war forced them to take to best perform their duty. Desperate for love, the children seek out their parents. They descend wildly for a loving and fatal and final embrace.

"The Children" was a minor Internet hit. A number of comics and pop culture blogs reposted it, and I received more than a hundred emails asking me to post the next chapter. The problem was that there was no next chapter. I attempted to oblige. Working in Najwan's style, I started a second chapter about the doctor who invented the machine that horrifically transformed the children, but I possessed neither the courage to commit the deception of publishing my work in Najwan's name nor the motivation to publish it under my own name. Soon, the reposts of Najwan's comics were limited exclusively to the memorial site, wemissyounaj. ca, started by Najwan's best friend. The comments on this site never ventured beyond superficial recollections like "OMG she was soooo talented." Out of frustration, I finally shut the comic blog down, though you can still find samples of Najwan's work on We Miss You Naj, which continues to act as a forum for her friends and former classmates to post poems of celebration and lament, MS Paint tributes, personal remembrances, and favourite photos digitally appended with condolences ("May our memories be our comfort") or famous quotes ("When a great woman dies, for years the light she leaves behind her lies on the paths of men").

No one has told the story that needs to be told. I had always thought that someone else would. I was absolutely certain that I was not the only one who had been completely changed by Najwan's murder and the events that led to it. I believed that I would not be the only person who was haunted by Najwan and Tom. But the truth is, we were a world. The three us were a world and I am now the only inhabitant left, the lone survivor, the last man, with nothing left to do but write, word for word, word by word, the origins of the world that was, which are the origins of our world's end. The envelope is less a miraculous sign and more a stern reminder: I'm it. The only one. The one I was waiting for is me.

I WAS SUPPOSED to attend an AGO symposium today, *Inside the Outsider Artist*, and speak as part of roundtable titled, "Comic Books from the Margins." I had promised in the summer to give a talk on *Sown Ayu*, or *Year Zero*, a comic composed during the Cambodian Genocide that documented the horrors of the Khmer Rouge's reign of terror. The comic was created by an anonymous collective of imprisoned artists who went by the name, New People, a term the ruling regime used to distinguish professionals, academics, and urbanites from the Old – rural, true, ideal – People. The KCP's attitude to the New People is best summed up by the motto: "To keep you is no benefit. To destroy you is no loss." *Year Zero* would have been banished to oblivion had it not ended up in the hands of a formerly KCP-sympathetic Western journalist who fled the country in 1976. The journalist had had the comic translated and distributed in an effort to shake the west out of its apathy toward the incomprehensible massacre. The original is preserved at a former high school-turned-death-camp-turned-museum in Phnom Penh, and both the 1977 translation and 1989 reprint are valued by serious collectors and thus quite rare. This past summer, all three of my attempts to purchase *Year Zero* turned out to be dead-ends, and before I had a chance to investigate further the Fall semester consumed me. I completely forgot about my AGO talk until a week ago, when a promotional e-vite, complete with a poster with my name on it, reminded me of my promise and my search for *Year Zero* began anew.

Before receiving the envelope, I had actually intended to attend the symposium. In place of the talk on *Year Zero*, I was going to give my usual talk on my own work, *The Swipe*, which adopted an intentionally "outsider" or *art brut* style. The Swipe was a parody of the teenager-turned-reluctant-superhero genre. My unassuming teen journalist, Sterling Stoops, was transformed into The Swipe after sneaking past a police barricade to shoot exclusive footage of his university's telecommunications research facility consumed by flames. The fire grew in ferocity as Stoops made his way to the roof, and then, just as Stoops got the shot he wanted of a blazing satellite dish, the facility exploded. Though the explosion evaporated Stoops' body, his consciousness was melded with his camcorder. The Stoops-Camcorder hybrid possessed the power to briefly steal, or "swipe," the form and function of any living thing or inanimate object. The catch: this "swipe" could only take place when an external user pointed the camcorder at said object or being and clicked "Record." I wanted the comic itself to mirror its hero, so I composed it entirely with "swipes." I copied (and modified, of course, for the sake of continuity and copyright) characters, panels, and full page layouts from great strips and comics, often mashing up eras and heroes, Winsor McCay with Jack Kirby, Astro Boy with Archie Andrews, to illustrate The Swipe's epic quest to find a permanent human form while thwarting the evil machinations of his growing rogues gallery: Mr. Original, Mage Marginal, and Supraman.

Instead of attending the AGO symposium and giving a talk on my old work, though, I committed to telling Naj's story. I retrieved my box of her things from the storage room, rearranged my office, dumped a file folder of unused quizzes into the recycling bin and started to file the materials from Tom's notebook. Skipping from this task to that task, penning "To Do" list after "To Do" list, I got this image of myself as a flock of sparrows alighting on the pavement, as though they were cast there like two handfuls of dice, landing in some truly ordered randomness and then hopping their hollow-boned selves from morsel to morsel, pecking at crumbs, coins, cigarette butts, the dried poo of other fowl, their multiple hungers combining to form a single feasting beast. I was so involved in my work that I did not feel a single drop of perspiration's worth of guilt over not having called the symposium's organizer at the AGO to say I was bailing, though I did finally turn my cell phone off, the intervals between its rings diminishing as my three o'clock talk neared. I tacked up Najwan's letter on the bulletin board to the right of my desk. I half-emptied and quarter-arranged the materials from the BCW comic box. I sat down to write this to you.

As I conclude these initial remarks, and prepare to begin telling Najwan's story, I realize that it was slightly deceptive of me to note that the card in the envelope was written the day before Najwan was murdered. My statement implied that she knew exactly what was coming. It implied that she was helpless and passive, writing to me as though I were her only hope. She did, of course, know something bad was coming her way, that was why she tried to leave the city, but she wrote the card, and asked me to return Tom's notebook, because she was cutting ties with the past, saying goodbye for good. Though her final note to me is brief, there is a confidence in the voice and lightness in the tone that suggests she truly believed she was almost in the clear. For the first time she felt like she was finally able to begin.

While I was writing to you, *Year One* arrived. My landline rang, I buzzed the UPS guy up, and he delivered a parcel that contained thirty-one copies of the Cambodian comic. It turns out that an error in the credit card info I entered the first time around had stopped the initial order from going through. The seller in L.A. had sent the thirty-one copies in response to my second order. Apparently, in between the threats and insults that constituted that toxic email, I had sarcastically remarked that his top-notch business probably only processed high-volume orders so I said I needed a copy for every day of the coming month. The seller had obliged. He even included an invoice to show that I had been charged for each copy, and a note that asked, "How's this for next fucking day?" The parcel had taken two days, but that fact did not diminish his overall point.

Though I am finally committed to telling you Najwan's story, I will have to take a break tonight to read *Year Zero* (though "read," I realize, is not the right word). I could hardly resist paging through it when I first opened the parcel. I just looked through it again. It's all here in pencil, preserved firsthand. The forced exodus. The forced labour. The force-less teachers and monks and civil servants and literates and artists and merchants and families forced into the fields, force-fed mottos: "The sick are victims of their own imagination," "Better to kill an innocent by mistake than spare an enemy by mistake." Water, fire, tool – the base elements of civil life and biological order are turned against life and order, in the name of life and order. Stories are forced, forcefully transcribed, and then the confessions are signed at gunpoint and then the gun is fired. It's all here, though sometimes sketched so quickly the panels and pain are seamed in senseless abstraction.

I am more than a little sickened to think I'd so carelessly offered to illuminate what should only steer us straight into pitch black. Any talk I might have given would have paled before what I'm looking at, the way hearing the word "moon" pales before feeling the moon fall from the sky and crush you where you sleep. This is the kind of work (wail?) that gets you thinking about the miracle of its creation (not the right phrase) and you feel (wrong verb, I know) like you're having your lungs pulled out through your oesophagus. It's the kind of thing you read (wrong) and wonder (wrong) how you will ever (wrong) at yourself in the (wrong) again.

On the Notoriously Overrated Powers of Voice in Fiction: or How to Fail at Talking¹ to Pretty Girls

D.W. WILSON

ON A TUESDAY afternoon in July, not too long ago, a friend of mine struck a pose imitating a self-portrait of the psychedelic Italian painter Pontormo. We were having lunch on a patch of grass outside some library near Russell Square. In his self-portrait, a goatee'd Pontormo levels one sweaty finger at the fourth wall, his hips half-cocked and his closest leg a little kinked, the whole thing oozing sex and transgression. Picture Johnny Depp meets Ewan McGregor. Picture dolled-up sixteenth century facial hair. Now picture: *speedo*, because that's all Pontormo's wearing – that and an expression that says he knows it. My friend (call her Annabel) was not wearing only-a-speedo, but I still felt a lump in my throat as if I'd swallowed a beating heart. I thought about telling her how good she looked, but I thought about a lot of things: how the hell I'd ended up in London, 7000 kilometres from home; how a train stays on its tracks by sheer friction; why the Victorians ever thought it a good idea to import a tree that smells like semen.² Mostly, though – at least, that Tuesday in July – I thought about ways to talk to

---

1   Throughout, I will shamelessly equate *talking* with *voice*, and potentially *dialogue*, in order to make this essay reek less of angst and desperation.

2   *Pyrus Calleryana* – no joke.

Annabel. I'm a fiction writer by trade, a modest purveyor of sweeping narrative, reticent dialogue, and moments of emotional revelation, but like a story never translates seamlessly from idea to paper, so too does it not translate seamlessly from paper to voice. Take that from somebody who knows.

Those seeking a tale of romance and bared hearts should seek elsewhere, because this is an essay on voice, not girls. Or rather, this is an essay on the poor comparison of voice and talking, and possibly on the failure of translation between the two – though in the examples to follow, the latter is nobody's fault but my own.

I'm going to make a bold claim and say voice is one of the most cited but least understood stylistic elements that readers respond to in fiction. Name a few good books and you'll find someone raving about the voice. Off the cuff: Ford's *Sportswriter*, David Mitchell's *Black Swan Green*, Andrew O'Hagan's book about a talking dog.[3] Publishers and agents stress the importance of finding 'new voices' (*Granta* devotes a section with that very name, every online issue, to an as-yet-unknown writer), and in creative writing workshops students are told they do or do not yet have 'their voice' by teachers who have or have not yet found theirs. Stories have voices and writers have their own, body-of-work voices, and writers also *talk* (apparently quite badly, if I am anything like a reliable cross-section). Meanwhile, academics gesticulate their theories about postmodernism and the deconstruction of the Self as a stand-in for saying anything at all.[4]

---

3   That book would be *The Life and Opinions of Maf the Dog and His Friend Marilyn Monroe*.

4   Insert thinly-veiled frustration with the Academy, here.

Voice is not talking – the written word being an inherently silent medium.[5] We say we like the *sound* of a writer's voice, but this is purely metaphorical, this is hand-waving, this is gross simplification of the highest order. What we actually like is some analogue of sound in a writer's voice, some approximation of how the voice-as-written represents the voice-as-spoken. Thoughts don't make noise.[6] The rhythms of a sentence shift between psychic and verbal. My favourite spoken word is *herringboned*, but my favourite written word is *syzygy*. Writing is a visual medium but also a cerebral medium; talking is almost wholly aural. I can't stress this enough – the gap between voice-as-written and voice-as-spoken is nothing short of ontological. The way I like the 'sound' of a writer's written voice shares no commonality with, for instance, the way I like the *sound* of Annabel's voice (here's the fiction writer in me, building tension).[7] There's more to voice than semantic field, diction, and rhythm (though that's certainly part of it) just as there's more to talking than the words that tumble from my mouth sans forethought – there's gesture, intonation, sound, stutter, stammer, and slip.[8]

So Annabel struck a pose and I felt as though someone was pressing a thumb to the divot where my breastbone meets neck. I've been taught to avoid judgments when writing fiction, so words like *gorgeous, pretty, beautiful,*

---

5   The clever cynic will say, —Ah ha! St. Augustine was mystified to find Ambrose reading silently! But my point is that there is a difference of *kind* between spoken and written words.

6   Look at a sentence written in an alphabet you don't understand, and you can't even begin to 'sound out' the words.

7   An opportune time to mention that she's British; I'm a small-town Canadian redneck.

8   Freudian.

goddess-of-my-idolatry get to taste my steeltoes[9] but let me
say this: Annabel is the kind of girl bumblebees try to gather
pollen from. Annabel is the kind of girl who boys write short
stories about. She's got reddish, brown-blonde hair (I'm terrible at these things) that cusps her jugular, green eyes with
a speck (I don't know what to call except a *speck*) in one iris.
She stands slightly taller than me but I try to make up for it
by donning a ballcap. Though I'd likely beat her in an arm
wrestle (I consider myself an expert arm-wrestler) she has
biceps that can manoeuvre the movement of a mare. When
she speaks, I am drawn to the motion of her upper lip against
her teeth – a motion I've also noticed in conversation with
other Brits. She wears shoes with small maple-leaf tags sticking from the sides, says they're reliable, tough.

We'd been editing each other's stories over lunch. Being
a thorough and thoughtful editor is basically my only skill,
and let me stress how difficult it is to turn that into a mechanism for inciting romance. She praised the voice in my story
and I praised her use of dialogue, and then she ridiculed me
for including a German Shepherd named Wolfhound, which
I have subsequently named after her, for revenge. Now,
though, she'd glided to her feet and struck a pose, and, with
this pose, the time had come for our lunch amid the semen
trees to end (she had work to do, is a biographer). Up until
that point I'd been summoning the wherewithal to voice
my attraction to her, but all lunch I'd found myself tongue-
tied, writer-blocked, had suffered a ball-gagging of the mind,
and the realization that she was now *leaving* caused in me a
certain degree of distress. Things I noticed, all at once: two
people with their backs to some statue of a horseman (the
British go crazy over these things) who looked too similar

---

9   I'm also a former electrician.

to be lovers, unless they'd been together for decades; the way Annabel grinned slyly down at me, her summery dress a-flutter; my notebook, arm's reach away, wherein I'd written a dialogue that outlined the way our conversation might go, the things I might say (I just like hearing you *talk*; nobody's feedback is as good as yours; I have a pretty big crush on you; wanna get a drink?).

In part, perhaps, I can blame my failure to talk (a failure of suaveness – *vastly* unlike me) on displacement, on sub-mersion in a country that sounds so different from the small town of my boyhood. I can blame it on being overworked, maybe: there's such a variation of dialect here, and nobody talks the same (at least not to my untrained ear) and there are all these nuances I'm blind to, gestures and conventions everybody takes so seriously but won't spend a minute to explain.[10] It's almost like trying to have a conversation from underwater. That, or I'm smitten by Annabel. But this dif-ficulty with voice does not extend to UK fiction; pick up a book by any British author, such as *Black Swan Green*, and except for points where David Mitchell is using vernacular or explicitly evoking a speech pattern ('Phelps dashed by, clutching his master's peanut Yorkie and a can of Tizer' – whatever that means), we read it in something approximat-ing our habitual voice. Reviewers rave about the narrator's voice in *Black Swan Green*, but if we're all 'hearing' a differ-ent voice for those same words, how – really, *how* – can we all enjoy it?

Canadian writers, Annabel has teased me, are less con-cerned with 'who am I?' and more concerned with 'where

---

10   The British journalist Sam Kiley tells me I have abysmal table manners, which comes as somewhat of a shock because I consider myself a well-mannered Canadian, and because we were eating pizza *with our hands*.

am I?'[11] Though I agree with her (or, though I can't easily defend myself against her[12]), I think the concepts of *where* and *who* cannot be so easily differentiated (what does it mean to be *Canadian*? To hail from Canada? To identify *self* with *place*?), but I do think where exerts much more influence on who than who does on where. Evidence to support this claim: pluck a small-town west coast boy from his home and plant him amid a society of people who take pride in their ability to pronounce things wrong (Wymondham becomes *wind-um*; Costessey becomes *cossy*; Happisburgh becomes *haze-bruh*). Then, watch. Things that'll happen: he'll wear his ballcap as if to safeguard his Canadianism from threat; he'll, bizarrely, develop a far greater interest in hockey than ever before; he'll score funding to do a PhD on 'Voice in Fiction' and be often criticized for his use of Canadian vernacular.[13] And he'll *actually* write a fictionalized dialogue between himself and a girl he has a crush on, and expect things to work out fine.

Here is a sample of the aforementioned exchange, scribed as I would scribe it in fiction:

—I've been getting so much work done, I said.

—Me too.

I looked across my shoulder at her. She'd turned aside, so I saw her in profile. A strand of her hair had tugged lose, so she pulled it behind her ear. She'd bunched the ends of her shirt sleeves in her fists, to keep her hands warm – bad circulation, I guess.

---

11 She is paraphrasing the writer Alberto Manguel, from his book *Reading Pictures*.

12 She is stronger than she looks.

13 Insert thinly veiled frustration with the Academy, here.

—Partly, it's because of all the writing games we've done, I said. —And partly because I've got a massive crush on you.

She chewed on that one for a second, tore up some grass and broke the blades in two. She seemed to consider them, like searching for answers, like throwing bones. —Why does that help?

—I don't know. Maybe it's like a siphon.

—A siphon? she said.

—Like, I siphon inspiration from you.

—Why?

—*Well*, I said, and pressed my hands to my chest, sounding as grandiose as possible. —Because you're so good looking.

She rolled her eyes, but it was the right kind of rolling of eyes.

I WON'T BOTHER transcribing the rest. It's one part embarrassment and one part fantasy.[14] I will, however, draw attention to the voice – not because I think there's anything particularly special about it (there really isn't), but because there are a number of voices to draw attention to. The characters in that passage have voices, and the narrator has a voice, and I – the writer, here, the scribe – have my own voice, and, reading that passage, the reader has her own, habitual reading voice. There are other voices too, layers of them: the Annabel character, the differences in how the reader will 'hear' her voice, how I, the writer, 'hear' her voice – did you read her with a British accent? And then there's the desperate male character, whose voice is something like an approximation of my real voice (and, mind-blowingly, so is *this entire essay*). One might be tempted by – and

---

14   Take your mind out of the gutter.

forgiven for – the notion that spoken voice and written voice are more closely related than they appear. They might also (especially if they're 25, and Canadian, and fumbling about for romance) be tempted by the notion that what reads well written down must sound good spoken aloud (say, in a park outside some library in London) but the *raison d'etre* of this essay is to dispel any such illusion.

Annabel and I left the park so I could walk her to the library. We crossed streets and our hips bumped, and I didn't know what to think, but I rarely know what to think. On the way, she showed me what she called 'the worst art gallery in London' and berated a hackneyed copy of a better painter's form. —It's like reading somebody trying to do Raymond Carver, and doing it badly, she told me when I said I didn't get it. —Look at the skin on the forehead – that doesn't look like real skin, that looks like *paper*.[15, 16]

But I was hardly listening at this point. Soon we'd part ways and I wouldn't see her for weeks, since, at the time, I didn't live in London, was only there to see my agent and to see Annabel, and the ambiguity of that which I had not voiced would drive me batshit ('Anticipation,' Frank Bascombe says, in Richard Ford's *The Sportswriter*, 'is that sweet pain to know whatever's next – a must for any real writer').

—There's something else, I said, deviating from script even at the starter's pistol. —Part of the reason I've been getting so much work done is that I've got a pretty big crush on you.

I felt, more than saw, her draw a breath, and of those few awful moments what I remember most keenly (though it is

15 Bet you forgot the British accent, bet you read that in your habitual voice.
16 Unless you, dear reader, are British, or your habitual voice is British. In which case: bet you forgot aboot my Canadian accent.

impossible, is my imagination) is her smell – like clean air, or the vague scent of flowers that is all flowers at once, and none at all. —I sort of suspected, Annabel said, and jittered a hand in front of her face. —I'm just, I don't know.

—Must've been obvious all along, I said.

—I'm pretty unaware. It comes from going to an all-girls school. Blind to things I don't want to hear. Not that I don't want to hear this. I'm glad you told me.

—Me too, I guess, I said. —It didn't quite turn out as I planned.

—What was your plan?

—Well you'd reciprocate and then I'd kiss you. I hope this doesn't make anything awkward.

People pushed by us. The streets were tiny, cobbled, the sidewalks tinier. Annabel swayed. I readjusted the weight of my pack. —I'm just not really looking for a relationship right now, she said. —I live in this bubble, and there are other people in this bubble, and the Pontormo thing.

Then a homeless man appeared beside us, with clothes all greys and greens and a dolled-up goatee. —Can you spare some change? he said, something for which I will never forgive him.

—I've only got my card, mate.

—Thanks anyway, he said.

—Wonder why he didn't ask me, Annabel said, after he left.

—Because I look like a dumb tourist.

—Yeah, she said.

We walked the rest of the way, to the back of the library. —Hope I haven't sabotaged you getting work done this afternoon, I said.

—You probably have.

—In that case we might as well go get a drink.

—Later, she said, but it was just to humour me. —I'm glad you told me, anyway.

—Self-preservation. I'd have lost my mind.

We stood there so awkwardly that against every instinct in my body I just wished the afternoon would end. And then I remembered a line from a short story of mine, a story about a determined and lonely man, which Annabel had read, and liked[17] ('If you lose all hope,' Frank Bascombe says, 'you can always find it again').

—Persistence beats resistance, I told her, quoting myself – which, I hope, illustrates (or, perhaps, undermines) the exact, bizarre nature of what we mean when we talk about Voice in Fiction, since what we've got *here* is my real written voice quoting my real spoken voice quoting my fictional written voice. And then telling you just that.

The problem, if I may make a bold claim – which, after all, is how I began this essay – is that critics and readers refer to voice as though it is an embedded thing, a physical part of the writing, as though you can point at an open book and say, —Here is the voice, I enjoy its girth. But I'm not convinced voice is a *thing* at all. I think it's an *act*, a passage of breath, a movement of sound, a certain transfer of meaning – the one special feature of writing that bridges the lonely gap between writer and reader, speaker and listener, lover and lover. Voice is the sensation of being soothed, of growing close, coming to trust. Second only to faces, it's how we identify people. Voice is authenticity embodied, but is itself unembodied; it does not exist if a story is not being read, if a person is not talking. It is transient, communicatory, interpersonal, *social*. Voice, I think, is the name we give to the creation of intimacy in our art.

---

17   'The Persistence,' from *Once You Break a Knuckle*. Shameless self-plug.

Annabel stopped in the entrance to the library, did a little back-and-forth tilt of her head (*I'll take it*, I bet she was thinking) and then, *therrapp*ing her fingers on the library wall, she leaned in for a hug. —Persistence beats resistance, she said to me, and rolled her eyes, but it was the right kind of rolling of eyes.

Upping the Anti

EZRA WINTON

Of Starfish and Jellyfish

"ISN'T IT BETTER to have a lot of people seeing films that convince them to make a little bit of change, instead of only a few people seeing films that may or may not convince them to make big changes?" This question was posed to me one summer evening by an emergency room (ER) doctor, at a rooftop gathering of "adjusted adults" – my term for people around my age but with handsome incomes, summer cottages, vacation plans and mainstream or centre-left political viewpoints. Folks, in other words, who don't make activist documentaries nor organize screenings of them.

I was describing my research to the doctor who, amicability aside, I had immediately pegged as a liberal and therefore fitting for my political posturing. Speaking of the current state of affairs of documentary and political activism in Canada, I then focused on the sad lot of radical and progressive political documentaries and their exclusion from populist mainstream currents, those elusive platforms and showcases where liberal documentaries are thriving like jellyfish.

I further developed the metaphor to clarify the situation.

Radical political docs are starfish: tough, plucky creatures destined to call home the sediment that forms from the activities of more prosperous organisms, forming small clustered communities of their own. Looking up through the shafts of luminous beams that ignite the circulation of free-moving and ubiquitous jellyfish above, stationary starfish behold their larger, limber liberal cousins.

Respected in their own communities, but mostly invisible to mainstream currents, radical political docs and doc-makers must constantly negotiate the uncertain waters of market exclusion, while the creators of less challenging works swim successfully in the larger lakes and oceans of mainstream culture.

I told the doctor that the continued marginalization of radical documentaries was deeply troubling, and not just for me, but for the planet. Returning my urgency with his own provocation, my jellyfish-supporting interlocutor summoned the formidable liberal consensus, and with well-meaning affectation, laid bare the challenge for all struggling starfish everywhere. If the radical politics and (he assumed) scrappy delivery of such docs didn't appeal to the masses, why fight for the starfish of the documentary world?

As futile as the rooftop debate probably was – my position remains the same and it's unlikely the doctor is spending his long hours in emergency considering my critical perspective – it does serve to demonstrate the seemingly intractable difference between a comfortable majority and an unsettled minority, the latter of which is enraged by the status quo and engaged in dismantling it. Following the moonlit gathering and still thinking about documentary, these two poles of cultural politics reminded me of the holy trinity of Canada's popular complacency of comfort, immunity and the dreaded consensus.

But, you may be wondering, what does the all rooftop ruckus and marine metaphors have to do with documentary and (dismantling) capitalism?

Resisting Resilience

WITH GLOBAL CAPITALISM in a protracted, full-fledged crisis, an opportunity has opened up for the airing of dissenting views, alternative perspectives, and critical dialogue on how our socio-economic system is structured. This timely opportunity continues to be squandered by the status quo – supporting mainstream and corporate media, much to the dismay of socialists, anti-capitalists and anarchists everywhere. So while the global elite pulls up its sullied socks and bails out the billionaires whilst further burdening the billions beneath them, alternative media is more important than ever. And while documentary itself can be argued to be an alternative medium, within the genre a mainstream centre is forming, with increasingly disconnected margins – the alternative edges of an alternative, if you will.

Despite its roots in state propaganda, banal educative endeavours and clunky television journals, documentary also rests firmly on a legacy of social justice, anti-oppression and free expression. Where mainstream journalism/ entertainment regimes have betrayed Finley Peter Dunne's maxim to "comfort the afflicted and afflict the comfortable," documentary has in many cases held up its end of the bargain. As author and academic John Downing (who teaches alternative media and social movements) says, documentary has "shone light on the crimes of the powerful, and portrayed resistance struggles against their dominance."

Yet not all documentaries are *afflicting* to the same effect, nor with equal solidarity, spirit and rigour against the status quo. In fact, many documentaries trade on social justice and resistance themes while they deliver tepid political analysis, showcase mainstream perspectives, and call for resilience or reform. The folks at Participant Media call this "social action entertainment." I call it liberal consensus documentary. Semantics aside, this raft of docs makes for a formidable school of jellyfish. And while I do not discount the role centre-left media has to play in building a fair and just society, I'm concerned recent jellyfish population blooms may be blocking out the sun for the radical starfish as they search to find their own currents. That is to say, I'm concerned for documentary's radical voices and their potential to be drowned out by the genre's own mainstream clamour.

Impact and Engagement

I WOULDN'T BE concerned about the "liberal" jellyfish if I didn't believe in the power of documentary to make a real impact on society.

Documentaries make claims on the real, or on actuality, while admitting to a degree of creative manipulation. As communication artifacts indelibly linked to notions of "truth," documentaries compel us to believe what we see and hear, to bear witness to what is recorded, and to relate to the representation of reality as it unfolds. As well, Professor Belinda Smaill of Monash University in Melbourne, Australia, reminds us that documentaries not only produce subjects, they also "construct documentary viewers who are equally implicated in a politics of the emotions."

As such, documentaries are ideal vehicles for intimating aspects of social reality unfamiliar or previously misrepresented, where we can be moved – politically and emotionally – by the language of cinema, into all kinds of post-screening actions. Documentary can provide the antidote to both apathy and ignorance, while stimulating a response from audiences that activates fundamental and even radical social change.

If mainstream and corporate media embody and exercise the power of influence, persuasion and consensus-building, then documentary, as an alternative media, can act as counter-power to that force. By chipping away at the dominant discursive veneer and exposing grand narratives as controlling mythologies of subjugation, documentary can activate a process of identification, diversification and community building.

Still, as someone who has been permanently changed from more than one documentary experience, I am aware that the call-to-action varies wildly, from changing light bulbs (*An Inconvenient Truth*, dir. Davis Guggenheim, 2006) to dismantling the corporate carbon trade system (*The Carbon Rush*, dir. Amy Miller, 2011) in order to combat climate change. There are vastly divergent strains in the political non-fiction genus – the species variations of what I call "take-action documentaries" – that translate and affect the equation differently.

There are three parts to my observations concerning take action documentaries in the contemporary Canadian landscape: (1) These "issue films," as they are sometimes called, can be partitioned off into two camps – *radical committed documentaries* and *liberal consensus documentaries* – with innumerable works swimming and drifting in the muddy waters between; (2) The latter type, the liberal consensus variety, has over time (and most significantly in the last two decades) become the dominant archetype of socially-engaged non-fiction cinema, especially in the programming of cultural institutions like film festivals and public broadcasters; and finally (3) Because radical and progressive perspectives are increasingly marginalized by the mainstream, commercial-friendly take-action documentaries and their attendant "small act" campaigns, a dominant discourse associated with liberalism – that of "doing good" incrementally, with an emphasis on instrumental critiques of social problems (bad apples, not rotten barrels) – has become ossified as the "take away" germane to the activist documentary screening experience.

Radical Committed Liberal Consensus Documentary

AMONG DOCUMENTARIES CONCERNED with socio-political issues and subjects, some tend toward a more populist, liberal and feel-good variety, such as *Waiting for Superman* (dir. Davis Guggenheim, 2010), while others tend to be more radical (in form and/or argument), and are inclined to challenge, implicate and confront (subjects and audiences), such as *Kanehsatake: 270 Years of Resistance* (dir. Alanis Obomsawin, 1993). When considering political take-action docs, I plot works along a constellation of political, cultural and social considerations, where radical films populate one end and liberal works, the other. Among such collections are films that activate and intervene in dominant regimes of knowledge, politics and culture – I call these "radical committed documentaries." Nearby are films that conform to perceived consensus and seek to provide audiences with aesthetic and political pleasure while usually calling for incremental reform. These are the "liberal consensus documentaries."

While both kinds connect with communities and put forward varied calls-to-action, they comprise significantly different perspectives, politics and desired outcomes. For instance, on the topic of drug addiction and poverty a radical committed documentary may put forward a critique of a socioeconomic system that produces massive social inequity, such as *The House I Live In* (dir. Eugene Jarecki, 2012); alternately this kind of doc may humanize and lend agency to an addict as she or he struggles to overcome multiple societal barriers, such as *Fix: The Story of an Addicted City* (2002) by Nettie Wild. In both cases, micro and macro aspects of society are presented as interconnected, and strong POVs are presented in ways that enable filmed subjects and activist communities to then leverage the documentary for their own agendas, thus contributing to structural and even radical social change.

The populist cousin to these docs, the liberal consensus documentary, is more likely to provide a framework focused on the personal habits of drug users and their seemingly innate inability to pull themselves up off their feet. In this case a micro-approach makes invisible the structural elements of social reality that connects the banker to the dealer to the judge to the user. These kinds of documentaries rely on emotional impact to connect with audiences, who are usually encouraged to take action in small, individual and therefore non-structural or radical ways, such as "talking to your children about drugs." Alternately, the "action" is to simply feel sorry for the subjects portrayed on screen. The depressing observational documentary *Sickfuckpeople* (dir. Juri Rechinsky, 2013), with its representation of child addicts surviving underground in Kiev, could be placed in this category, as could the 1999 NFB doc *Through a Blue Lens* (dir. Veronica Alice Mannix), which is unfortunately still used in secondary education curriculum throughout Canada.

The liberal consensus message is thus articulated along lines of inclusion and exclusion, where the audience is not really part of the "world" of those on the screen. In the projected other world, drug use and therefore addiction is concerned with personal choice and it's therefore up to the individual to make the right or wrong decision. The complex web of geopolitical economics and culture that produces drugs, drug culture, legal frameworks and drug users is reduced to the individual actor, and does not implicate the non-addict. This *disconnectedness* is part of the mythology of the liberal consensus documentary, and it is one that fits snugly with the dominant philosophy and social order of deliberative democracy that serves the ideological needs of capitalism. You are the source of your misery. The individual is the agent of change. Focus on the small act.

Radical committed documentaries are works that dually activate and intervene in said dominant social orders and accompanying ideological frameworks. They are activist films that are used organizationally and in campaigns. Unlike liberal docs, they are not ends in and of themselves. They are communication efforts unafraid of articulating a strong POV, and are deployed to radically transform our social order and underlying socio-political and economic structure.

Radical works are concerned with activating audiences and intervening in mainstream, status quo structures and hierarchies of power. They often implicate audiences by evaluating an issue structurally, and suggest that problems are collective and interconnected, not individual and isolated. This includes implicating powerful and elite factions of society like the police, government and dominant institutions while at the same time involving audiences. This can be an uncomfortable experience, as anyone who has watched *The Act of Killing* (dir. Joshua Oppenheimer, 2012) can attest.

Liberalism's Troika

Comfort

RETURNING TO THE elemental triumvirate of Canadian liberalism, we can see that the two documentary types approach storytelling, meaning-making and social action in very different ways. Where radical committed documentaries are disruptions in the mainstream flow of culture, politics and media, and therefore seek to dislodge our sense of complacency and comfort, liberal consensus docs seek to entertain, draw audiences in through familiar associations and uphold a general wellbeing shared among an imagined *adjusted adult* demographic. *The Cove* (dir. Louis Psihoyos, 2009) is an excellent example of a political take-action doc that does not seek to disrupt the comfort of its intended Western audiences – whom it does not burden nor implicate – but instead crafts a 'boys with toys' narrative of espionage and intrigue that plays into a perceived consumer-oriented middle-class audience familiar with James Bond fiction. At the end it is the Japanese who are at fault, as well as the international regulatory bodies, while the collective audience sitting in a theatre in Toronto or New York remain disconnected.

Immunity

COMFORT LEVELS ARE connected to the notion of immunity versus complicity. The best radical committed documentaries implicate both the ruling class and the audience members, which can cause great discomfort to the viewers. The idea of immunity is reinforced in liberal consensus documentaries, where audiences are sacred (the consumer is king!) and should not be made complicit in systems of harm, injustice or inequity, other than as minor players who are powerless to the larger political machinery that shapes their social reality.

Liberal consensus documentaries, at their worst, reinforce regimes of harm and inequity by upholding the status quo, especially when they give complicit power elite platforms to champion dominant narratives. Any radical committed documentary worth its salt would not give problematic figures like Condoleezza Rice (who appears in *Miss Representation*, dir. Jennifer Siebel, 2011) or Bill Clinton (who is featured in *Fire in the Blood*, dir. Dylan Mohan Gray, 2012) screen time to shape their PR image into caring, philanthropic individuals who contribute to female empowerment and HIV/AIDS drug accessibility, respectively. In both these cases, the end justifies the means: famous personalities, despite political baggage, will help guarantee a bigger audience for the product. These compromises around complicity are part and parcel of the liberal consensus documentary, a form that seeks to reform dominant social order structures, not dismantle the status quo of which those interviewees are card-carrying members.

Immunity in this sense is a social condition whereby the logic of exclusion informs a rhetoric of blame (in liberal consensus docs) that does not implicate either side of the system but bestows agency to individual choice-makers, who are capable of effecting small change. This impulse is so powerful in recent documentary cinema that Hot Docs 2010, inspired by the inclusion in the festival's program of the Swedish documentary *A Small Act* (dir. Jennifer Arnold), created a whole sidebar devoted to the idea. By providing inspirational, emotional and positive stories of individual philanthropy, films like *A Small Act* tunnel in on individuals "doing good" and reinforce our own potential to make isolated contributions to the betterment of our social condition.

At the same time, these films do not offer any kind of structural critique. No one asks why the schoolteacher in Sweden, who generously pays for a Kenyan child's education, is living in such comfort while the Kenyan child is living in poverty. There is no pause to reflect on the connection between such contrasting economic realities. In films like *A Small Act*, Western audiences aren't implicated in the larger system of global inequality. They're engaged instead in a positive association with the Swedish teacher whose small act contributes to the wellbeing of a distant other. The consensus is maintained. The status quo is left intact.

Consensus

WHICH BRINGS ME to the last of the three elements of liberalism expressed in the liberal consensus documentary. Chantal Mouffe has written extensively on consensus as the liberal fantasy connected to deliberative democracy, whereby sustained rational dialogue and debate will produce a consensus on any issue. Those of us living in the real world simply know this isn't the case, as I was reminded of on that rooftop talking to the doctor. Mainstream and corporate media help manufacture consensus, to paraphrase Chomsky, by shaping the conversation and setting the agenda for what are – and aren't – the important discussion topics and issues. Watching CTV or CBC news, for instance, reveals a very narrow, superficial and almost ridiculous perspective on what we, as Canadians, should consider important issues and topics. With the rise of reality TV, infotainment and now "social action entertainment," ripples of non-fiction consensus-making now contribute to mainstream journalism and corporate entertainment's agenda to uphold the status quo and protect the comfortable who are in the business of afflicting.

For their part, liberal consensus documentaries reinforce meta-narratives and overarching systems of social organization. The poorly made and intellectually vapid documentary *POM Wonderful Presents: The Greatest Movie Ever Sold* (dir. Morgan Spurlock, 2011) is a good example of consensus in liberal documentary. While the film trades on activist impulses and promises a critical examination of the marketing/PR world, it ultimately serves to uphold the status quo of crass commercialism, free market capitalism and the commodification of culture. Corporate media and affiliated cultural/political institutions uphold the status quo around the industrial entertainment complex, and part of that dominant narrative is the marketing of democracy as fuelled by the power of the individual consumer and their choice. *POM* offers no critique of this system and instead serves the industry a feature-length promotional video that stole screen time from better political docs on the festival circuit and during a lacklustre theatrical run.

Conclusion

SO IF THE ER doctor isn't going to watch any radical documentaries, shouldn't everyone just abandon ship and bob with the jellyfish? Aren't the starfish destined to remain bemired in obscurity?

Comfort thrives on distraction and entertainment. Immunity thrives on individualism. Consensus thrives on ignorance and apathy. To combat liberalism's troika and to not only *imagine* a fair, just and sustainable world, we need alternative media like radical committed docs that will push farther than the documentary mainstream fare currently nudges. But without audiences, these films become even less effective than their liberal consensus counterparts.

I am hopeful that radical independent non-fiction cinema can combat and correct the mainstream media tide of consensus and its normative reinforcement of systems of domination and exploitation, capitalism included. But two challenges must be faced head on.

1. Working With and Around the Liberal Consensus Documentary

THE JELLYFISH POPULATION and its reach grow daily. While I do not completely dismiss this kind of filmmaking and I certainly enjoy an entertaining socially conscious film like anyone else, these kinds of documentaries are proliferating inside funding envelopes, on television (what's left of it) and in film festivals. All the while, the starfish languish.

This is happening as eviscerated public media are compelled toward private commercial models or extinction, as a political climate elevates a liberal/conservative so-called middle ground on every issue, and as documentary filmmakers adopt commercial, populist models of education-entertainment. As audiences and critical publics we need to put more pressure on filmmakers to kick harder against the pricks. Their films will be better for it, and our communities engaged in dismantling the status quo will be better for it.

It should go without saying, but related to this is the need to support those organisms in the murky nether-regions of our vast media ocean. Radical, activist, anti-corporate and anarchist film festivals are out there and would love to see you! If there isn't one nearby, look up some programming and find ways to support the documentaries that resonate with the kind of change you want to see. As audiences our horizons will be broadened, our resolve deepened and our knowledge, well you get the point. As radical, committed artists facing all kinds of obstacles, the filmmakers get much-needed support.

2. Building and Supporting Linking Agents

WHILE THERE MAY be an abundance of quality, progressive and radical socio-political documentaries out there, the unfortunate flip side is that there is a huge lack of linking agents, with regard to distribution and dissemination. For radical committed documentaries to have the greatest impact and help in campaigns and social movements to enact change, they need to be seen by more people in the right context. With the twin movements to commercialize and put documentaries online, we should be wary of losing fertile connections to grassroots, civil society and activist organizations and campaigns. Initiatives like the in-development UK Radical Film Network not only help films by generating buzz, they continue the work of the docs by expanding the filmic worlds of subjects, pushing issues into the public sphere and directly connecting with take-away and plug-in community and civil society actions.

Festivals could serve this function, but the large commercial festivals are focused on the jellyfish and their own professional propagation. Documentary fans, makers and enthusiasts need to build a sustainable set of platforms for radical committed documentaries to educate, engage and impact, and we need to work together to develop a culture of appreciation and support for these works, especially by familiarizing young media users who often do not have a priori enculturation, and therefore interest, to access these works.

Never before has so much information been available to so many, yet the commercial media and their political-economic support systems continue to pollute our waters, making it difficult to find the starfish and nurture their communities. Capitalism is in crisis, and never before have its managers and benefactors been so vulnerable to attack, while its dissenters and detractors so poised for charting a new course. Yet, here we sit, drowning in information, barely able to see through the plumes of jellyfish, those well-meaning organisms that have adapted with a strategy of resilience, while the rebellious starfish still search for ways to puncture the status quo boat above, as it slightly rocks from light liberal lunges.

On the rooftops or in the sea, I'll be looking for the starfish and supporting their ascension to the surface. Unless, of course, I get distracted by that new doc series about nifty eco-products...

Author Biographies

MARION AGNEW's fiction and creative non-fiction has been supported by the Ontario Arts Council and has appeared in literary journals in the U.S. and Canada. Her essay, "All I Can Say," was shortlisted for the 2009 CBC Literary Awards and appeared in *Best Canadian Essays 2012*. She lives and writes in Shuniah, near Thunder Bay, Ontario (www.marionagnew.ca).

AARON BROVERMAN is a freelance writer based in Toronto, Ontario by way of Surrey, B.C. His work has appeared both online and in print for such publications as *Investment Executive*, *Financial Post Business*, *Askmen*, CBC, *Huffington Post Canada*, *Eye Weekly*, *Nerve*, *Bankrate*, *DigitalSpy*, *Moviefone* and *Walletpop Canada*, among others.

HEATHER CROMARTY received her B.A. in English from the University of Calgary and promptly moved to Toronto, where she's lived for over a decade. She is a reviewer and critic for *Lemon Hound*, *Quill and Quire*, and *The Globe and Mail*, among others.

SARAH DE LEEUW is a two-time recipient of a CBC Literary Prize for her creative non-fiction essays, and is the author of three literary books, one of which (*Geographies of a Lover*) won the 2013 Dorothy Livesay Award for the best book of poetry in British Columbia that year. She is a geographer and creative writer who, as faculty in the Northern Medical Program of UBC's Faculty of Medicine, teaches and undertakes research about medical humanities and colonialism. She lives in Prince George, BC.

STACEY MAY FOWLES is an award-winning novelist and essayist whose writing has appeared in numerous anthologies, including *Yes Means Yes, Finding the Words,* and *Nobody Passes.* Her bylines include *The Walrus, The National Post, Elle Canada, The Toast, Deadspin, Jezebel, Rookie, Hazlitt, Quill and Quire,* and *Worn Journal.* Her latest novel, *Infidelity,* is out currently with ECW Press and was named an Amazon best book of the year.

NAOMI K. LEWIS is the associate editor of *Alberta Views.* She is also the co-editor of *Shy: An Anthology* (UAP, 2013).

LEWIS MACLEOD teaches in the English Department at Trent University, with an interest in Modern and Post-Modern cultures and literature. His work has appeared in a variety of journals in Canada, the United States and the U.K. He has also played in a number of bands; his most recent recording is *For Sale As Is.*

MARGO PFEIFF is a Quebec-based journalist and photographer with a special passion for the Canadian North which she has visited more than two dozen times in the past 20 years.

ANN SHIN is a writer, new media producer and award-winning filmmaker. Her latest cross-platform project is *The Defector: Escape from North Korea*. Her second book of poetry, *The Family China*, was published by Brick Books in 2014.

KILBY SMITH-MCGREGOR's fiction has appeared in *Brick, Descant, Web Conjunctions*, and been recognized by the Writers' Trust of Canada with the RBC Bronwen Wallace Award. Her nonfiction has appeared in *Brick* and in *The Kenyon Review*. Kilby will publish her first collection of poetry with Wolsak & Wynn's Buckrider Books imprint in 2016.

EUGENE STICKLAND was Alberta Theatre Projects' playwright-in-residence for 10 years and a *Calgary Herald* arts columnist for five.

KATE TAYLOR is a cultural critic and novelist who writes about the arts for the *Globe and Mail*. In 2009–10, she was awarded the Atkinson Fellowship to study Canadian cultural sovereignty in the digital age, publishing the results in the *Toronto Star*. Her 2003 novel, *Mme Proust and the Kosher Kitchen*, won the Commonwealth Writers' Prize for best first book (Canada / Caribbean region) and the Toronto Book Award. Her second novel, *A Man in Uniform*, was published in 2010; she's currently writing a third.

RICHARD TELEKY is a Professor in the Humanities Department of York University and the author of eight books, including novels, short fiction, poetry and critical studies. His most recent books are *The Dog on the Bed*, which explores the human-dog bond and its representations, and *The Hermit in Arcadia*, a new collection of poems.

DANIEL SCOTT TYSDAL is the author of three books of poetry, *Fauxccasional Poems* (forthcoming from Icehouse 2015), *The Mourner's Book of Albums* (Tightrope 2010), and *Predicting the Next Big Advertising Breakthrough Using a Potentially Dangerous Method* (Coteau 2006). His poetry textbook, *The Writing Moment: A Practical Guide to Creating Poems*, was recently published by Oxford University Press. He is a Senior Lecturer in the Department of English at the University of Toronto Scarborough.

D. W. WILSON is the author of the short story collection, *Once You Break a Knuckle*, and the novel, *Ballistics*. His fiction and essays have appeared in literary magazines in Canada, Ireland, and the United Kingdom, and he is the recipient of the 2011 BBC National Short Story Award for "The Dead Roads." *Ballistics* (Bloomsbury UK & US, Penguin Canada) was selected for the Waterstones Eleven and longlisted for the Dylan Thomas Prize.

EZRA WINTON is the co-founder, with Svetla Turnin, of Canada's largest grassroots documentary screening network, Cinema Politica. He holds a PhD in Communication from Carleton University and teaches alternative media, media and social movements, and cinema. He is also a contributing editor at *POV Magazine* and *Art Threat* and his last major publication was the volume he co-edited with Thomas Waugh and Michael Brendan Baker, *Challenge for Change: Activist Documentary* at the National Film Board of Canada.

Permission Acknowledgements

Grateful acknowledgment is made to the following for permission to reprint previously published material:

"Words" appeared in *Room* 36.2 © copyright 2013 by Marion Agnew. Used with permission of author.

"Canadian Caped Crusaders" appeared in *This Magazine* (July/August 2013) © copyright 2013 by Aaron Broverman. Used with permission of author.

Review of Amber Dawn's 'How Poetry Saved My Life' appeared in *lemonhound.com* (June 2013) © copyright 2013 by Heather Cromarty. Used with permission of author.

"After Paul Auster Spoke About Lightning" appeared in *Filling Station* 55 © copyright 2013 by Sarah de Leeuw. Used with permission of author.

"Boy Next Door" appeared in *Walrus* (Dec 2013) 55 © copyright 2013 by Stacey May Fowles. Used with permission of author.

"On the Notoriously Overrated Powers of Voice in Fiction" appeared in *The New Quarterly* 125.4 © copyright 2013 by D.W. Wilson. "On the Overrated Powers of Voice in Fiction" was originally published internationally in *The White Review* #1 (2011). Used with permission of author.

"Upping the Anti" appeared in *POV* 92 (Winter 2013) © copyright 2013 by Ezra Winton. Used with permission of author.

Editor Biographies

CHRISTOPHER DODA is a critic, editor, and poet from Toronto. He is the author of the poetry collections *Aesthetics Lesson* and *Among Ruins*, and his poems and reviews have appeared in journals and magazines across Canada and internationally.

NATALIE ZINA WALSCHOTS is a poet and a music journalist who writes about heavy metal, CanLit, speculative fiction and horror, feminism, combat sports and video games. Her work has appeared in *The National Post*, *Quill & Quire*, *The Globe and Mail*, *Rue Morgue*, *Game Dynamo*, *Torontoist*, and *Exclaim!* Her second book of poetry, *DOOM: Love Poems for Supervillains*, was published by Insomniac Press in 2012 and her first, *Thumbscrews*, won the inaugural Robert Kroetsch Award for Innovative Poetry. She lives in Montreal.